Restoring Hearts Journal Through Your Process

By Stephanie Daniels

Stephanie Daniels

Introduction

The Spirit of the Lord is upon me, because He hath anointed me to preach the gospel to the poor; He hath sent me to heal the brokenhearted, to preach deliverance to the captives, and recovering of sight to the blind, to set at liberty them that are bruised, to preach the acceptable year of the Lord.

Luke 4: 18-19 KJV

Restoring Hearts- Every human being was created to commune and fellowship with God. Without intimacy with God, the cares of this life will leave us broken and downcast. Jesus died to bridge the gap between God and man. Now He is resurrected sitting at the right hand of the Father. We are instructed to cast our cares on Him. Through salvation, Jesus has equipped us with everything we need to be victorious in life. No matter what we go through, we can hold our heads high and walk with purpose into our destiny. Jesus is the lover of our soul. He has set the captives free and healed the broken hearted. Consider journaling as you read Restoring Hearts. Allow the Lord to minister to you in a way that you can later reflect on and share with others. Stay blessed and encouraged.

Dedication

To the Heart Restorer, my Lord and Savior, Jesus Christ.

Table of Contents

Introduction: 3

Dedication: 4

Chapter 1-True Intimacy: 8

Chapter 2-God Can Use You: 28

Chapter 3-The Army of the Lord: 32

Chapter 4- Stay on the Path: 38

Chapter 5-Intercession: 46

Chapter 6-Fellowship: 49

Chapter 7-Seek First the Kingdom: 52

Chapter 8-Get to Know Yourself: 57

Chapter 9-Lifestyle of Worship: 68

Chapter 10-Get a Vision for Success: 80

Chapter 11-Habit Forming: 91

Chapter 12-Build a Bridge to Your Success: 106

Chapter 13-Use Your Authority: 115

Chapter 14-Reinforce Your Bridge: 127

Chapter 15- Start Moving Forward: 135

Chapter 16-Stay on Track: 145

Chapter 17-Take Someone with You: 153

Chapter 18-Celebrate Your Victory: 161

Chapter 19-Maintenance: 168

Chapter 20-Process to Promotion: 176

Lifestyle of Prayer: 181

About the Author: 183

Chapter 1

True Intimacy

God created each of us with a desire for intimacy. Intimacy means different things to different people. The word intimacy is defined as: Intrinsic; suggesting informal warmth or privacy; of a very personal or private nature. (Source: The Merriam-Webster Dictionary) The first thing most people think of when they hear the word intimacy in our culture is sexual fulfillment. While there is a level of intimacy achieved between two people when they come together sexually, *true intimacy* is achieved through the cultivation of a spiritual relationship with God. Those that worship God must worship Him in spirit and in truth. John 4:24 NKJ

We find the greatest and most fulfilling love ever known to man is when we seek God with our whole heart and lean not on our own understanding. Proverbs 3:5 NKJ

God is love. He loves because that's who He is. You were created to be loved, to experience love at the highest level, with the one, true, living God. Love never fails. God is always faithful. We have an enemy named Satan who roams around like a roaring lion seeking whom he may devour. 1 Peter 5:8 NKJ

Satan is the author of confusion, but God is the author and finisher of our faith. Hebrews 12:2 NKJ

Satan has studied mankind since the days of Adam and Eve. He understands the power we possess when we believe in, lean on and trust our Heavenly Father. Satan comes to steal, kill and destroy. John 10:10 AMP

One of his strategies is to use manipulation and lies to push people into the wrong way of thinking about God. Once this is achieved, there is an open door for the enemy to lead that person into sin, doubt and unbelief. Trusting God comes when a person makes a conscious decision to walk by faith and not by sight. Faith comes by hearing and hearing by the word of God. Romans 10:17 NKJ

The only way to develop a healthy relationship with God the creator of Heaven and earth is to accept Jesus Christ as your Lord and Savior and spend time in prayer and His Word. In the beginning was the Word and the Word was with God and the Word was God. John1:1 NKJ

The Word of God is the ultimate guide for mankind. It is the absolute truth. Many people don't want to believe in an absolute truth, because that means giving up their own opinions and choosing to believe what the Creator of Heaven and earth says about any given topic. His Word tells us to believe in our heart and to confess with our mouth that Jesus is Lord. Romans 10:9 NKJ

Believing anything else is a lie, but it is also a choice. People were given free will and the ability to choose. Heaven is full of people who made the right choice. We wouldn't know what God required, if it were not recorded in His Holy Word. God chose the Jewish people to preserve His Holy Scriptures. It explains how Jesus Christ died for our sins and how the Holy Spirit is our comforter. You and I can read and study His will and His ways for ourselves. For thou art a holy people unto the Lord thy God: The Lord thy God hath chosen thee to be a special people unto Himself, above all people that are upon the face of the earth. Deuteronomy 7:6

The life of Jesus is the perfect picture of love personified. Jesus left His glorified position in Heaven and humbly came to earth, through a virgin named Mary. And in the sixth month the angel Gabriel was sent from God unto a city of Galilee, named Nazareth, to a virgin espoused to a man whose name was Joseph, of the house of David; and the virgin's name was Mary. And the angel came in unto her, and said, "Hail, thou that art highly favored, the Lord is with thee. Blessed art thou among women." And when she saw him, she was troubled at his saying, and cast in her mind what manner of salutation this should be. And the angel said unto her, "Fear not, Mary: for thou hast found favor with God. And, behold, thou shalt conceive in thy womb, and bring forth a son, and shalt call his name Jesus." Luke 1:26-31 KJV

Jesus lived a sinless and powerful life going about doing the will of His Heavenly Father. Jesus healed the sick, raised the dead, cleansed the lepers, turned water into wine, preached good tidings to the poor and did many other powerful things to fulfill the will of God on the earth. He took the time to make disciples and instructed them to do even greater works than He did. He explained how He had to return to the Father but would send His Holy Spirit as a Comforter. God the Father, God the Son and God the Holy Spirit are one. Their functions are intertwined just as we are a spirit. We have a soul and live in a body. For I came down from heaven, not to do mine own will, but the will of Him that sent Me. John 6:38 KJV

Now that I've established the foundation of what love is and where love comes from. Let's talk about *your love life*. You will always feel empty and unfulfilled, until you fill the void in your heart with the one, true, living God. So many times we seek fulfillment through others. God created us to be relational creatures. In His Word, He said, "It is not good that man should be alone; I will make him a helper comparable to him." Genesis 2:18 NKJ

God has no displeasure in giving you meaningful and loving relationships with others, but He will not allow you to put them or anything else before Himself. We, as humans, can sometimes short change ourselves by putting things such as spouses, careers, positions, fortune, fame or anything above God.

Success should not be rated on the outward appearance of a person's situation. We can all think of people who we may have viewed as successful, only to hear of a tragic, untimely ending to their life. Suicide is from the enemy. Satan is the father of lies. He makes promises he can't keep. He then bankrupts the person who gave in spiritually, emotionally, mentally and/or physically. But the Lord said to Samuel, "Do not look at his appearance or at his physical stature, because I have refused him. For the Lord does not see as man sees; for man looks at the outward appearance, but the Lord looks at the heart." 1Samuel 16:7 NKJ

Don't starve your spirit! We are a spirit. We have a soul and we live in a body. Most people have no problem taking care of their flesh. They groom it with expensive oils, lotions and colognes. They feed it things like steak, lobster, caviar and even chocolate mousse then they exercise their flesh. They purchase several gym memberships where they can jog, run, or walk on the treadmill for hours.

They dress it up with designer clothing. They have dozens of shoes and beautiful jewelry. We can't forget about sex. Many people will satisfy their flesh sexually outside the will of God, which is marriage between one man and one woman. Sex is a beautiful gift from God that comforts and satisfies, but when it is used outside the will of God, it becomes a weapon against your own body. Flee sexual immorality. Every sin that a man does is outside the body, but he who commits sexual immorality sins against his own body. 1Corinthians 6:18 NKJ

All this is for the flesh that will eventually return to dust. Some people care about their soul enough to get counseling, if they feel they need it. They look to self-help books and the philosophies of man, searching for earthly wisdom to satisfy the soulish part of their being. Unfortunately, all of those same people will find themselves at a crossroad in life sooner or later and won't know which path to take.

The reason for this is because we must be led by the Spirit of God. They spent their life neglecting the most important part of themselves, the part that is eternal. Our soul will spend eternity in one of two places, Heaven or hell. We should feed our spirit the Word of God, daily.

Speaking in tongues is a powerful gift from God. Praying in the spirit in an unknown tongue to manifest the perfect will of God is privilege. Some people don't want this free gift of power. We should be careful what we expose ourselves to in the world, but be open to the things of God. We must study to show ourselves approved rightly diving the Word of Truth. If we don't study God's Word, we won't know what is good and acceptable to Him. They have become more open to the things of God. To God, be the glory. Guard your heart above all else, for it determines the course of your life. Proverbs 4:23 NLT

Our spiritual walk is the most important part of our human experience. We live in a natural world, but God has super natural love and blessings that He wants to pour down unto each and every one of us. Then Peter opened his mouth, and said, "of a truth I perceive that God is no respecter of persons:" Acts 10:34 NKJ

What He has done for one, He will do for another. The difference between the one who walks in the blessing and the one that does not is a matter of a willing and obedient heart and/or the individual's belief system. Remember, I said earlier, man looks at the outward appearance but God is always examining the heart. He knows what you will do before you do it. He also knows why you do what you do. When God asked Adam and Eve where they were in the Garden of Eden, He knew. The question was for them to come to a realization of how far they had fallen. While some people have a willingness to live according to the will of God and are obedient to what God says to them, there are others who rebel and use their free will to do as they please. Rebellion of Godly principles always leads to destruction. There are still others who desire to please God, but have wrong mindsets that have been sown into them. Somewhere along the way, they were deceived. God makes provision for these people by His Holy Word. My sheep hear My voice, and I know them, and they follow Me. John 10:27

The Word of God also makes it clear that the enemy can't pluck God's children from His hand. God speaks your language. If you being evil know how to give good gifts to your children, how much more will your Father, who is in Heaven give good things to those who ask Him! Matt 7:11 NKJ

What do you think? If a man owns a hundred sheep, and one of them wanders away, will he not leave the ninety-nine on the hills and go to look for the one that wandered off? Matt 18:12 NIV

One thing that I feel impressed upon to discuss are some of the ways the enemy may twist or distort a person's thinking about relationship with God. Some people have been groomed to see God as a mean, old father in the sky throwing lightning bolts at anyone who does wrong. This distorted view is designed to make some people give up on a relationship with God, feeling they would never be good enough to satisfy an angry God. The good news is that God is not mad at you! He wants you to come in alignment with His great plans for your life.

I know the plans I think toward you says the Lord, plans to prosper you and not harm you, to give you an expected end. Jeremiah 29.11 NKJ

There are many distorted views, but I'll humbly share a wrong view of God that gripped my thinking for years. I had a negative self- image which made me view God in the wrong way. Allow me to use a poetic version of my testimony for this illustration.

Stephanie Daniels

What My Father Did for Me

In the Heart of God is where I started, (Jer.1:5)

I feel like a part of me never departed.

He wrapped my spirit in flesh and sent me on my way,

I was born in NYC on a cold winter's day.

He predestined me for victory. He had a purpose and a

plan. (Jer. 29:11)

He accounted for my sins and equipped me to stand.

He knew there would be times that I would stumble and

even fall.

He lovingly reminded me to repent and stand tall.

He constantly whispered, you're equipped to succeed,

But when I looked into my mirror, I didn't like what I did

see.

He taught me that His Word is what reveals my true

reflection,

And that I am connected to His love and protection.

As I journeyed through my life seeking His will and His

ways,

He loved me unconditionally each and every day.

As His plan for ministry unfolded in my life,

(Mark 16:15)

He revealed to me that I would also be a wife.

But woe unto me, my joy turned to sorrow.

When God's will tarried, I lost hope for tomorrow.

I started to ponder why there was a delay.

I realized it was that I needed to pray.

I tried to bring God's will to pass,

But nothing I did in the flesh would last.

Stephanie Daniels

Hope deferred makes the heart sick,

(Proverbs 13:12)

But God had the ultimate fix.

My wounded heart was restored,

His blessings in my life can't be ignored.

God's Word as my mirror, showed me the real me,

And that my end result would be a complete victory.

The Holy Spirit stayed close as a faithful friend.

I will serve Him until the end.

God's true love restored me.

He was right on time.

The Holy Spirit whispered love was always mine.

God is the Restorer of my heart

and the Lover of my soul.

Jesus is the One who makes me whole.

I'm going to worship and forever will I praise,

The love of God will surely amaze.

Jesus is the King of Kings, (1Tim.6:15)

(Rev.19:16)

He has created everything. (Gen: 1:1)

He is closer than a brother and a lifelong friend,

His love is eternal. It will never end.

Jesus is our soon and coming King, seeking His bride,

I'll be ready and waiting, love never denied.

I got off the path, because I started to seek after the promise more than the Promise Giver. This caused confusion to come into my life. When the enemy comes in like a flood, the Lord raises up a standard against him. Isaiah 59:19 NKJ

Have you ever taken a detour and struggled to get back on course? Some detours can turn into a maze of twist and turns and forks in the road. We have to rely on our Holy Ghost GPS. He is always with us. He will never leave nor forsake us, but we can grieve Him with our choices. Spend time in prayer and be led by the true Leader. God is the Leader. Children love to play follow the leader. God wants us to follow Him through obeying His Word and standing on His promises with childlike faith. He can't fail us.

He has never failed and never will. This is a hard concept for some people. They see with their natural eyes the failures of men and they also see their own failures. They struggle to see God's perfection because they have their eyes on themselves. It is true, we can do nothing of value in our own strength, but there is nothing impossible **with** God! There is nothing He doesn't understand or hasn't taken into account. His love is an unfailing love. *His ways are fair and just.* He is all seeing, all knowing and He is everywhere. God is the great I Am. What then shall we say to these things, If God is for us, who can be against us? Romans 8:31 NKJ

There is no way to talk about *restored hearts* without talking about forgiveness. The Word tells us to forgive. For if you forgive men their trespasses, your Heavenly Father will also forgive you. But if you do not forgive men their trespasses, neither will your Father forgive your trespasses. Matt 6:14-15 NKJ

Oftentimes, forgiveness has to start with ourselves. Forgiving and uncovering truth about oneself can be painful. God wants everyone to be victorious in their life choices. It was painful for me to admit that I was living my life in a self-sabotaging mode. I wanted to find someone or something to blame my lack of life's success on. When I was able to turn my pointer finger honestly to myself, I became aware that I was accountable for what happened in my life. What an empowering moment! This revelation set me free, but it took some time to reverse some wrong mindsets.

Jesus also leads by example. His life is a love walk. In the book of Acts, Peter explains how Jesus is no respecter of person. He tells us that Jesus went about healing all that were oppressed by the devil. Acts 10:38

The key to this verse is that little three letter word, **ALL**. Jesus showed compassion and healed all manner of sickness and disease. He only required faith. That is all that is required of you and me. Some people have faith in the wrong things. Jesus is the only way. There is no other way to the Father. If you confess with your mouth and believe in your heart that Jesus is Lord you shall be saved. Romans 10:9 NKJ

As Jesus made His way to the Cross, He had converted many people into believers. The ultimate act of dying on the Cross was the greatest love ever shown. For God so loved the world that He gave His only begotten Son, so that whoever should believe in Him would be saved and have ever lasting life. John 3:16 NKJ

Jesus is the only way to the Father.

Start your heart restoring journal, by journaling your thoughts about intimacy with God. List some ways you can cultivate your relationship with your Heavenly Father. If your life was a poem, what would it sound like? If your life was a picture, what would it look like? If your life were a song, what would be the melody?

_____

_____

_____

_____

_____

_____

Chapter 2

God Can Use You

There is a saying that one man's junk is another man's treasure. Sometimes, people can look like a lump of coal to you, because of the circumstances surrounding their life. God sees every soul as a valuable treasure. God loved us, while we were yet sinners. His love never fails, but the love of man can fail. If you fail to look a certain way or perform according to expectations, the love of man can wax cold. Remember, God is love, so we don't have that problem with Him. He is the Potter. We are the clay. He will continue to work on us as long as we are willing to stay on the Potter's wheel.

God is not only powerful, but He is the **power source**! Every resource in your life, every ability, talent, career and gift, every single resource comes from the source.

He is the Alpha and Omega, the First and the Last, the Beginning and the End. He holds all of creation in the palm of His hand. To know Him is to love Him. When you have an encounter with God Almighty you are never the same again. In His presence is fullness of joy and at His right hand, pleasure evermore. Psalm 16:11NKJ

God can use our junk to purge the junk from others. How can this occur? Let's look at the Apostle Peter. He was a man who was quick to spew out his opinions and quick to take action. Jesus told His disciples that He would be crucified on the Cross. Peter didn't want to agree with what God was saying because of his lack of understanding. Jesus stated, "Get thee behind me Satan." Matt 16:23 NKJ

Jesus wasn't calling Peter Satan, but He was speaking to the spirit that was influencing Peter's thinking. Now, the fact that the other disciples probably heard it and that we can read it today is just one example of how God can use our junk.

Peter went on to do great things in God, but he did have to be purged from some stinking thinking. God saw fit for us to read about this in His Holy Word. This could have easily been omitted from the Scriptures. God could have only referenced the good things that His people said and did and then told us to follow their example. Instead, God chose to allow us a look at the shortcomings of the men and women in the Bible to show us how He can still use any of us to do great things. This should be comforting information in your quest to get to know God more intimately. God is not looking for perfect people. He is looking for moldable people with a willing and obedient heart.

The people of Israel are God's chosen people, yet the Bible is full of scenarios where the people of Israel were called stiff necked and disobedient. God had to discipline them on many occasions. He turned them over to the hand of their enemies, but lovingly gathered them back to Himself.

Some people would view this as a lack of love. I beg to differ. The word states, "God chastens whom He loves." Proverbs 3:12 NKJ

What type of parent would never correct their child? Think about that for just a moment. If a child grows up without any correction, they are doomed to fail. Spare the rod, spoil the child. Proverbs 13:24 NKJ

Journal about some of your trash-to-treasure moments in life. We all have a serendipity story. What's yours?

_____

_____

_____

_____

_____

_____

_____

Chapter 3

The Army of the Lord

God's Army has an army. That's right! The Army of the Lord can call on angels at any time. In any thought out, well organized plan, there are levels of intelligence. You have ranks broken down into Privates, Corporals, Officers, Generals, etc. You also have different branches such as ground troops, army, air force, navy, marines, etc. and you have different divisions. Everyone has a specific task. Some may be strategic planners, some clean up hazardous waste, some police the area, etc. No matter which area you fall into in the Army of the Lord, you are very valuable. There is no unimportant job in the Army of the Lord or Body of Christ.

We, as the Body of Christ, only function properly when everyone is doing their part. In the military, there is a group called Special Forces. There are also groups in government, such as CIA (Central Intelligence Agency), FBI (Federal Bureau of Investigations) and DEA (Drug Enforcement Agency). They all deal with classified information. There are things that are considered to be on a need to know bases. God gave us everything we *need to know* in **His Word**. The Word of God is alive! Use your spiritual eyes and an open heart to learn something new each time you read it.

As a mature believer, you are given the keys to the Kingdom which is more information. A child is like a servant, until they grow up and are able to handle the keys to the Kingdom. Galatians 4:1 Paraphrase NKJ

A good parent doesn't turn over the car keys to a 5-year-old. A good parent nourishes and cares for a child until the age of maturity. A good parent will also leave an inheritance for their children's children. Proverbs 13:22 NKJ

The keys to the Kingdom are not given to spiritual babies, but to mature saints. Matt.16-19 Message version

Journal about the whole armor of God. List each piece of armor and write about how you use it in your life.

_____

_____

_____

_____

_____

_____

_____

_____

_____

_____

_____

_____

There is power in the House of God! God is Love. He is also Power. As I said earlier, He is not just powerful, **He is**

Power. The Holy Spirit is the source that we can all plug into for power. He requires us to get filled and refilled. It's not a onetime thing. We must continually be filled. I remember a time when my teenager invited her friend to our church. The friend came with her family and there was speaking in tongues going on before service began. The friend later told my daughter that she and her mother felt uncomfortable and that the speaking in tongues was weird. It's so interesting to me that the same people will pay to watch a horror movie and feel just fine. We have to be able to identify with what is good, what is right and what is true. We live in this world, but this is not our home. We must be Kingdom minded. Acts 2:2-4 NKJ

There is evidence, when a person has power in their life. Like we just said, the evidence of speaking in tongues is one of them, laying hands on the sick and seeing them recover, preaching the Gospel with fire and boldness, discernment, words of knowledge, words of wisdom, etc. are others. We shall know them by their fruit. Matt 7:15-20 NKJ

The fruit of the spirit should be evident in the lives of believers. The fruit of the Spirit is love, joy, peace, long suffering, gentleness, faith, meekness, temperance, against such there is no law. Gal 5:22 NKJ

God commands His people to love the Lord thy God with all your heart and love your neighbor as yourself. Luke 10:27 NKJ

Your love walk is the best example of God's power ruling and reining in your life. God's agenda is winning the lost. We should always be about our Father's Business. And He who wins souls is wise. Proverbs 11:30 NKJ

Are you plugged into the ultimate power source? Journal about a time God gave you supernatural strength to get through a difficult time.

_____

_____

_____

_____

_____

_____

_____

_____

_____

_____

_____

_____

_____

Chapter 4

Stay on the Path

There may be times in your life when you feel the urge to fall back. There may even be times when you get ahead of God. These are really bad ideas. It's important to walk with God, remembering He is the Leader. Remember, we talked about playing follow the leader as children. God wants childlike faith and obedience. Matt 18:3 (NKJ)

There is no big I and little you, in the Kingdom of God. We are all under the authority of Jesus Christ. When you've done all you can do, then it's simply time to stand on the Word. Some people get off track, because they are looking for a quick fix in life. Most people have a desire to feel successful and to receive acknowledgement for their accomplishments. Don't let your self-worth be in what you do. Your self -worth should be in who you are. You are a child of the one, true, living God. Walk worthy of this distinguished title. It calls for humility and discipline.

Is there anything or anyone in your life trying to pull you off the path that God has you on? Write about the situation in your journal. Seek God, for the solution.

_____

_____

_____

_____

_____

_____

_____

_____

_____

_____

_____

_____

_____

The true treasures in life are the things that moth and rust can't destroy. Desire spiritual gifts, wisdom, discernment, peace and favor. I learned to listen to the frequency of Heaven. The frequency of the world is stressful and alarming. The frequency of Heaven is joy and peace, because we have the victory in Christ our Lord. In order to come into the fullness of the treasures of Heaven, we must detox from the things of this world. Detox your mind, body and soul, through fasting and prayer. The prophet Daniel had a specific diet of healthy foods, avoiding the king's dainties. Daniel 1: 12 NKJ

At the end of his fast, he was healthy and looked good. I believe that his fast not only released treasure for him to spiritually discern, it also gave him strength, health and a good appearance. When we purpose in our hearts to press in to the things or take a stand for righteousness, God will move on our behalf.

While you're on the path to reaching your goal, be sure that you don't grow weary in the waiting season. Anything worth having is worth waiting for. But they that wait upon the Lord shall renew their strength; they shall mount up with wings as eagles; they shall run and not be weary; and they shall walk and not faint. Isaiah 40:31 KJV

God's reward is for those that endure until the end. Matt 24:13 NKJ

We have been called the "microwave age", because technology has allowed us to experience things at really fast speed. God's timing isn't always our timing. Long suffering is a fruit of the Spirit. Sometimes the wait seems long, but we have to be patient on our journey and wait for our breakthrough. Be not slothful, but followers of them who through faith and patience inherit the promise. Hebrews 6:12 (NKJ)

Allow me to illustrate a modern day scenario of what it means to not wait on God. A high school student recently shared with me a story about a young man from her high school. He was not very popular and occasionally was bullied. He went home and decided to make a contract with the devil, thinking he could have the prestige that he desired. He went to school the next day looking better and bragging about what he had done. The contract he claimed to have made with the devil stated that his life would end around 30 years old. That didn't seem to bother him. Meanwhile, this young man confided in a mutual friend that he had acquired an incurable STD during all of this. Now the enemy loves to make big promises, but the wages of sin is death. I believe there is still hope for this young man. I believe he can repent and turn back to the Lord.

I believe that just like the prodigal son, he can be healed and restored, but the key is he must make the decision to turn away from his sin and accept Jesus as his Lord. Luke 15:11-32 NKJ

The enemy has targeted the youth of today. One way he does this is through desensitizing. People, especially young people, get desensitized to sin by watching it, reading it and hearing it every day. This generation has the fastest access to information since the beginning of time. Unfortunately, most of the information is bad. For the wages of sin is death; but the Gift of God is eternal life through Jesus Christ our Lord. Romans 6:23 KJV

Call on the name of Jesus. Trust the Lord to deliver you out of trouble. "No weapon that is formed against thee shall prosper; and every tongue *that* shall rise against thee in judgment, thou shalt condemn. This *is* the heritage of the servants of the LORD, and their righteousness *is* of Me," says the LORD." Isaiah 54:17 KJV

As the scripture explains, trouble may come, but we can take authority over it as children of God. Spend time hidden in prayer, so that you can emerge strong and ready to overcome anything that tries to come against you. He that dwells in the secret place of the most High God shall abide under the shadow of the Almighty One. Psalm 91:1 NKJ

There are so many comforting scriptures to stand on in the day of trouble. God is able to open a window of Heaven over your life and pour out any source of provision, protection, or wisdom needed. Just ask Him. Remember, there is power in the Blood of Jesus. When the Israelites were leaving Egypt to enter the promise land, the death angel passed by the blood that they were commanded to put on their door. The Blood of Jesus is our security. God has also blessed us with angels that respond to our words of faith. Speak life over your situation and the circumstances of others.

Make a list of some things you need to detox from. Remember, everything in moderation.

_____

_____

_____

_____

_____

_____

_____

_____

_____

_____

_____

_____

_____

_____

_____

Chapter 5

Intercession

I once read a book by Joy Dawson entitled *Intercession Thrilling and Fulfilling*. I sowed the book into a friend, but kept the concepts in my heart. The book encourages the reader to stir up the gift of intercession. A strong prayer life is not optional to the life of a believer. It is mandatory for victory over the enemy.

Nothing happens, until we pray. There was a prophet named Elijah, who called fire down from Heaven. He dared his enemies to set up the altars to their pagan gods. He challenged them to see if their gods would come through for them. They wailed and cut themselves, jumping around foolishly, but nothing happened. Elijah suggested that maybe their gods were just sleeping. Elijah, then, went a step farther with his faith. He had water poured on his sacrifice.

The scene was set with a dripping, wet altar. Then the miracle came. Elijah called on the God of Israel and fire came down from Heaven and licked up all the water and the sacrifices of the pagan people. 2 Kings 1:9-10(Message Paraphrase)

This could only be accomplished, because the prophet Elijah had the ear of the Father through prayer. Elijah knew his God. He communed with his God. He obeyed his God and knew that if he asked in faith, God would move in his life. The enemy roams around *like* a lion seeking whom he may devour. He can't devour God's people of faith. Stand your ground. You have been given dominion and authority.

How much time do you spend in prayer each day? Do you pray for success and well-being of others? Don't forget to pray for the peace of Jerusalem.

_____

_____

_____

_____

_____

_____

_____

_____

_____

_____

_____

_____

Chapter 6

Fellowship

Spending time with God is crucial. Spending time in corporate prayer is also a great way to strengthen the believer. We are like iron sharpening iron. We are told not to forsake the assembling of the brethren. Hebrews 10:25NKJ

We are to hold each other accountable, while loving each other. Remember, we are the Army of the Lord. We are like a well-oiled machine. If a man be alone when he falls, who is there to help him up? Eccl 4:10 NKJ paraphrase

We should speak life and encouragement into the hearts and minds of each other. Prophecy is a great gift, because it edifies and builds up.

I recently started taking prayer walks while walking my granddaughter's dog. It's just a few minutes a day to take dominion and authority over our beautiful neighborhood. We all should plead the Blood of Jesus over our region and territory. Before we can truly walk in our God-given dominion and authority, we must make sure that we are walking in love and forgiveness. God's Word says to forgive, so that your Father in Heaven can forgive you. If you have alt with your brother, lay aside your offering, go and make it right with him and then, go before the Lord. Matt 5:23 NKJ paraphrase

Make sure the condition of your heart is addressed, if you aren't receiving desired results in prayer. God has blessed each of us with gifts and abilities. People can develop their natural talents, but spiritual gifts come from the Holy Spirit. Romans 12:6-8 KJV tells us that spiritual gifts are prophecy, ministry and exhorting. Speaking in tongues is another spiritual gift, as is the interpretation of tongues. Being able to give a word of knowledge is another. Use your gifts to glorify God. I try to use creative writing as a teaching tool to glorify God. The gifts of God are given without repentance. Romans 11:29 NKJ

Is God speaking to your heart about increasing your prayer life? Consider joining a prayer group. Seek God for direction.

_____

_____

_____

_____

_____

_____

_____

_____

_____

_____

Chapter 7

Seek First the Kingdom

If we are not careful, people, places and things can become our priority or focus. This should never be so in the life of a believer. We are to seek first the Kingdom of God and all His righteousness and these things shall be added unto us. Matthew 6:33 NKJ

Human beings were created with need, desire, preferences, opinions, etc. These are some of the things that make you uniquely you. However, there is one common need, hope and desire that we should have above no other. That is a hunger and thirst for intimacy with our Heavenly Father. God created us for relationship with Him. "I am the way the truth and the light, no one comes to the Father, but by Me," says the Lord. John 14:6 NKJ

Accepting Jesus Christ as your personal Lord and Savior is essential to a happy, victorious life. Victory means different things to different people. We should seek God's Word for His idea of victorious living. Many people can relate to the fact that sometimes bad things happen. Adam and Eve lived in a perfect place called the Garden of Eden. They had no sin and no worry, until they disobeyed God's command. In doing so, Adam gave his dominion to the devil. Jesus won back our victory on Calvary. There are still many who don't know this and allow the enemy to use them. We wrestle not against flesh and blood, but against principalities and rulers of wickedness in high places. Ephesians 6:12 NKJ

Don't get stuck in your past. We are new creatures in Christ. Old things have passed away and behold, all things have become new. 2 Corinthians 5:17 NKJ

The only one who wants you to beat yourself up over past sin and failure is Satan. He is the ultimate failure! He lost a position of beauty and power in Heaven. There is no redemption for him. He is condemned to hell and an eternity in the lake of fire. Don't go there with him! Jesus said, "I came that they might have life and have it more abundantly." John 10:10 NKJ

If you are a believer, you are saved from an eternity of separation from our loving, Heavenly Father. Repentance is a big deal with God. We are required to repent of sin in our lives. Repentance is being sorry and *turning away* from the sin. There is a Bible story, where the Pharisees set out to trick Jesus into doing or saying something wrong. The Pharisees were jealous of Jesus and, because of their greed and selfishness they didn't want people to believe in Him. They brought a woman, caught in the act of adultery, to Him and asked what should be done. Remember, Jesus was going around healing and forgiving people, so Jesus stooped down and began to write on the ground. The Bible doesn't tell us what He wrote, but I always pictured Him writing down the names of the men this woman had committed adultery with, which could have very well been the accusers. Jesus stood up from whatever He had written and said, "He who is without sin cast the first stone." John8:7 NKJ

Each Pharisee turned and made an exit. No one could condemn her after that. The woman was left alone with Jesus and He asked her, "Is there no one left of your accusers?" She said, "No Lord." He said, "Neither do I condemn you. Go and sin no more." The devil hates this! He hates that we can be forgiven. He is called the accuser of the brethren. He wants to temp you, lead you and condemn you! Don't let him. Tell the enemy, he is under your feet. He is a defeated foe. Remind him where he's going and tell him you won't be joining him!!! Share your faith with others and help them come to realization of who God is. Glory to God!!!

Leave the past in the past. It's a new day. Start thinking with a fresh perspective and be Kingdom minded. Ask God for witty ideas, not to make you famous or rich, but to advance the Kingdom of God! When He gives you the idea, write it down. God wants to use you.

Chapter 8

Get To Know Yourself

I spent most of my life not knowing who I was or what I wanted to do with my life. I did the foolish thing of comparing myself to others, only to fall short every time, because I wasn't them. I didn't realize the best part of being me was my God-given uniqueness. I firmly believe that styles, fads and trends are started by the creative people in the world that dare to be different. The rest of society then follows their lead, thus creating the latest trends. It's important to determine what makes you special in life. We all have God-given gifts and talents that were intended to be shared. You may sing, dance or create computer programs, but whatever you do, make sure you do the best job you can with it.

And whatsoever ye do, do it heartily, as to the Lord, and

not unto men; knowing that of the Lord, ye shall

receive the reward of the inheritance: for ye

serve the Lord Christ. Colossians 3:23-24 KJV

If you don't know what gifts and talents have been entrusted to you, start by doing something. You'll find a natural progression in the right direction, once you get busy for God. Procrastination is a sure road to nowhere. When you put effort into something, your creativity comes to life. You may start off in the mailroom and end up in the boardroom, but you'll never know until you try. The key is to purpose in your heart to start something positive in your life and watch it grow. I call this *farming your future*. We have to plant the seeds that we want to see grow in our lives. When they grow, they produce fruit. The results can be amazing.

I have to admit the fact that not only did I not know myself, but I didn't like myself. I was never a person who would intentionally harm anyone else, but I indulged in more than my share of self-sabotage. It could have been a job opportunity, relationship or some life experience that I would walk away from prematurely or held on to for dear life, when I should have let go. Now that I have learned to study myself through journaling, I can appreciate me being me. Every day I wake up and thank God for another chance to be the best me I can be.

This is the day which the Lord hath made; we will rejoice and be glad in it. Psalm 118:24

One area of self-sabotage I frequented was self-doubt. I never thought I was good enough, smart enough or attractive enough to do anything. I'm not saying that I never started anything. I'm saying that I never finished. The voice of self-doubt would convince me to walk away to avoid the shame of not being able to make it.

This type of negative self-talk caused me to fall short with many opportunities. It wasn't the culprit of every failure, but it was involved often enough. I grew into a tenacious person who would push through adverse circumstances to get what I wanted. My new attitude came later in life, but better late than never.

This journaling process is designed to assist you in defining, reaching and maintaining your life goals through self-awareness, using Godly principles. *Finding what makes you thrive and what makes you strive,* is one way to take authority over the circumstances surrounding your life. The fear of failure overwhelmed me most of my early life. The voice of doubt never told me that walking away from things prematurely would bring the very pain that I was trying to avoid. The spirit of fear made me feel unworthy of anything good, yet there was a part of me that believed *God had something special for me.*

For I know the thoughts that I think toward you, says the Lord, thoughts of peace, and not of evil, to give you an expected end. Jeremiah 29:11 KJV

Everyone has some amount of fear about something. When you determine what fear is present in your life, you can begin to eradicate that fear through applying God's Word to the situation.

For God hath not given us the spirit of fear; but of power, and of love, and of a sound mind. 2 Timothy 1:7 KJV

The first step to identifying fear triggers in your life is to set aside time in prayer. God delights in revealing answers to problems.

Be careful for nothing; but in everything, by prayer and supplication with thanksgiving, let your requests be made known unto God. Philippians 4:6 NKJ

Prayer time is so important, because it is communication with God. Pray without ceasing. Once you have direction, you can begin to journal. Go through a typical day and list key things that impacted your day. For example, did you begin your day with prayer? Did you wake up in a good mood? Did you wake up feeling rested and refreshed? If not, try to determine what type of thing interrupts your sleep. I will both lay me down in peace, and sleep: for thou, LORD, only makes me dwell in safety. Psalm 4:8

Were you able to communicate effectively during the day? What type of dietary choices did you make the day before? Were you able to incorporate exercise into your day? When you answer basic questions like these about yourself on a regular basis, you can begin to see what life adjustments need to be made. Once the adjustments are determined, you can begin to make positive changes in your life. Research one of the most important subjects in your life, *you!* Start by challenging yourself. Allow yourself to be honest and transparent in the journaling process. Journaling doesn't work if you're not honest. No fiction. Keep it real!

Note your short term goals by category: faith, family, career, etc. Choose a category and focus on the steps necessary to achieve that particular goal. For example, if you started with faith, perhaps you could challenge yourself to wake up 30 minutes early each morning for devotional time. Maybe you would choose to increase your alms giving. If you start with family, maybe you would discuss communications styles with your loved ones. Find out what is important to each member of the family. Sometimes, it's just making more time for family activities that bring the greatest joy to your loved ones.

If you start with career goals, it may be that you need to first assess your strengths and weaknesses to determine the career path that would work best for you.

Make sure you determine what motivates you during your journaling process. Are you driven by a high income, helping others or prestige? You must be honest with yourself for this type of journaling assessment to work. Train yourself to be motivated by pleasing God. Some people have trouble accepting the truth, especially when it's about them.

And ye shall know the truth, and the truth shall make you free. KJV

Today, I accept the truth of God's Word. I can accept the rod of correction, keeping in mind that I'm God's child and that He chastens those He loves. This is a truth that everyone should hold onto. It's so easy to be discouraged by personal failure, mistakes and shortcomings. These things are realities that can be changed by consistently applying the Word of God to your life. When we listen to the Holy Ghost with a willing and obedient heart, victory is inevitable. Create your best realty by surrendering your life to God.

Another self–sabotaging behavior that many people engage in is choosing the wrong relationships. When you don't recognize your own value, you tend to surround yourself with the wrong people. Don't allow critical or judgmental people to be a part of your inner circle and don't surround yourself with *yes men*. Find friends that are kind and willing to tell you the truth, in love. Do the same for them. No one wants to be criticized or ridiculed by the people in their life. You can avoid strife by following practical wisdom from the Word of God. A soft answer turned away wrath: but grievous words stir up anger. Proverbs 15:1 KJV

Why do we sometimes devalue what God has placed the highest value on? If God says we are fearfully and wonderfully made in His image, we should honor that. The more I got to know myself, the more I was able to forgive myself, love myself and keep myself accountable to the Word of God. This process involves studying the Word of God. I learned the Will of God through His Word. Study to show thyself approved rightly dividing the word of truth. KJV

Once I got to know myself, I got to know the good, the bad and the ugly. I have to admit that at first, it was too painful to honestly look at my shortcomings. I struggled with self-esteem issues all my life, but when I looked at myself with the perspective God had revealed through His Word, I saw that I was redeemed from the curse of the law. I was set free by the Blood of Jesus and clean in the sight of God. Reflecting on my past wasn't a place where God wanted me to camp out. I just needed to see where I came from and commit to God's way of life for my present and future.

Today, use your journal to help you identify your key values. Once you've narrowed down your list you will start to see things about yourself that you may not have been aware of.

What do you value? What are your short and long term goals? What makes you smile? These are just some of the questions you should know the answers to. Think about it for a moment and start journaling your thoughts.

_____

_____

_____

_____

_____

_____

_____

_____

Chapter 9

A lifestyle of Worship

A lifestyle of worship involves faith, obedience, and reverence. It took me some time to grasp this important concept. Once I embraced this truth, faith in God helped me to rise above the circumstances of life. I still had issues, but unlike in the past, I was able to overcome my issues. Obedience helped me to develop intimacy with the Lord. Without obedience, hypocrisy is inevitable. Reverence simply means that now I have a holy fear and respect for God and His Holy Word.

God is no respecter of persons. He loves us all the same. It sometimes seems that groups of people try to make God in their image to build their own sense of self-worth, instead of understanding that we are all made in His image. God loves us and created us with a purpose. But the very hairs of your head are all numbered. Mathew 10:30 KJV

He has a specific plan for each individual on the planet and His plan is good! So many people stray away from God's plans for their life because of their own selfish ambition, then they blame God when things go wrong.

Seek ye the LORD while He may be found, call ye upon Him while He is near. Isaiah 55:6 KJV

We have to embrace God and His plans in order to experience the fullness of Life that He desires us to have. You can start with getting to know God as Father and then, getting to know yourself. A relationship with God is the most valuable relationship a person can have. Jesus said,

"No one comes to the Father except by me." When we accept Jesus as Lord of our lives, it opens the door for intimacy with the Father. Born again believers have access to the Throne of Grace through the Spirit of God. We are to be constantly filled with the Holy Spirit of God in order to walk in power here on earth.

Have you ever wondered why some people clear a room within five minutes of entering it, while others have people flock to them? Have you ever stopped to think about what you bring into a relationship? Do you bring peace or war? Are you critical of others or compassionate? Do you dominate every conversation or are you an active listener? We all need to understand our personality style, what makes us tick and how we respond to others in various situations and circumstances. It's important to be honest with God and yourself.

I've always enjoyed studying psychology, but what became more fascinating is the newer trend of Life Coaching. Life Coaching originated with the Greeks. This concept of walking beside people in an effort to encourage and motivate them inspired me. I see that this is what Jesus did with the disciples. A strong mentor can be beneficial in the life of a new believer.

God is the best Coach, because He'll ask you questions about yourself that He already knows the answers to. He does this to help *you* learn about yourself. He did this with Adam and Eve when they disobeyed Him in the Garden of Eden. God asked Adam where he was. Adam stated he hid himself because he was naked. God then asked, "Who told you that you were naked?" God asked these questions to allow Adam and Eve to realize the answers. God knew what was going to happen before He formed the foundation of the world. He already had a plan for our redemption.

You also have to know your *spiritual temperature*.

The Holy Spirit discerns between the bone and marrow. KJV

He knows us better than we know ourselves. Take an honest assessment of your spirituality. Are you hot or cold? If you're hot, you are passionate about the things of God and put Him first. If you are cold, you don't care about the things of God. If you are lukewarm, you may have a form of godliness but deny the Power of God. God is passionate about us. Be passionate about Him. As with **any** relationship worth having, you must spend quality time cultivating it. A spouse that works all the time won't have a happy mate, nor will a worker who never listens to the boss's instructions. These are things we have to consider with God. He requires obedience and desires fellowship with us. Obedience and fellowship go hand in hand.

We are all given a measure of faith. That means every human being on this planet has the ability to believe. We all believe something, but do we believe the right thing? There are so many opinions on every subject under the sun. One fact remains, absolute truth is *absolute*. To believe anything but the truth is wrong. What is truth, you might be asking? Well, truth is the Word of God. Allow the Holy Spirit to lead you into all truth. It will take time and discipline, but it is so worth it. Ask God to lead you to the right church. Becoming a member of a church that teaches the Word of God is another way to get to know God. We are not to forsake the assembling of the brethren. We are like iron sharpening iron. Being around other spirit-filled believers strengthens us in our walk with the Lord.

Another important aspect of getting to know yourself is identifying your triggers. We all respond to stimuli differently. Some people think loud noise and blinking lights could mean there is a party nearby while others may see it as danger. You may associate a fragrance with a pleasant experience while the same smell produces migraine and or traumatic feelings in another person. There are some people who see a father figure as a leader, provider and friend while others see a father as cold, uncaring angry or absent. This is all based on the human experience. This concept can also be associated with many things and places in your life. For example, you may be in a toxic relationship or may find that living in a certain area drains your energy. Learning your triggers will help you make better life decisions.

There is good news about getting to know oneself. No matter what you discover about yourself, God has given you the power to change what needs to be changed, the power to forgive and the power to be forgiven. We don't have to strive to be something we're not. We can be the best version of ourselves through the Blood of *Jesus*. The only thing that stands between you and positive change in your life is you. Our enemies were defeated, when Jesus died on the cross and rose on the third day. Uncovering truth about oneself can be painful. It was hard for me to admit that I was living my life in a self-sabotage mode. I wanted to find someone or something to blame my lack of life success on. When I was able to turn my pointer finger honestly to myself, I became aware that I was accountable for what happened in my life. What an empowering moment! This revelation set me free, but it took some time. Having a victim mentality doesn't occur overnight and, yes, God can fix it in an instant, but most of the time He will allow His people to *walk it out through process*. What a cool God! He lets His people learn and grow all under the protection of His *grace and mercy.*

Be real with yourself. Remember, this process only works when we are willing to face the truth, whatever it may be. Let's look at a Biblical example. King David was a mighty warrior, a man after the heart of God. The Bible tells us that there was a time, while his army was out at war that he chose to stay behind. He noticed a beautiful woman, named Bathsheba, bathing. He summoned that woman to his castle and had his way with her. Bathsheba was the wife of Uriah.

David later had her husband killed to cover up his sin. When the priest came to speak with David, he gave him an analogy of a rich man who stole the beloved ewe lamb of a poor man. David was outraged and suggested that this man should be held accountable. The priest explained to David that he was that man. That was a painful truth to David. David had to face the fact that he had sinned and used extremely poor judgment. He had to admit the truth about himself. We must be able to, not only see the path that has led us astray, but to also turn from it.

When you get to know yourself, you can set goals for self-improvement and self-fulfillment that will help build self-esteem. Be sure to get to know the One who created you. It is crucial to develop your personal relationship with God. He holds the keys to your success and He wants to prepare you to live a victorious life. Set a standard for your life based on the Word of God. Don't compromise. When you make a mistake, learn from it, forgive yourself and move on. God is not standing around holding on to every mistake you make. He forgives those who seek His forgiveness.

For if ye forgive men their trespasses, your Heavenly Father will also forgive you. Matthew 6:14 KJV

The Apostle Peter was a great man of God. He started off like most believers, immature in his understanding of the Will of God. Jesus told him he was going to be betrayed into the hands of men. Peter said, "Not so Lord". Jesus then predicted that Peter would deny Him three times. Paraphrase Matthew 26-34 KJV

Peter later went on to become a great apostle. There was also a time when Jesus asked Peter if he loved Him three times in a row. Jesus knew Peter loved Him. Jesus was reinforcing the importance of spreading the Gospel, because each time He asked, He said, "Feed my sheep". At the end of Peter's life, he had ministered to many people. Peter's divinely inspired contribution to the Bible continues to minister to people today. When the Roman soldiers came to crucify him because of his faith, Peter felt that he was unworthy to be crucified in the same manner as Jesus, so he asked to be crucified upside down. These occasions in

Peter's life demonstrate Peter's spiritual temperature throughout his walk with the Lord. Peter was definitely hot!

True faith requires commitment. We have to love the Lord our God with all our heart and our neighbor as ourselves. It is not until we die to selfish ambition and put our lives in the hands of God, do we truly *start to live*. God is love. Living a life of love means that we are patient, kind and longsuffering with ourselves and others. This can be a hard pill to swallow in a "microwave generation", where people want things done yesterday. Who has time to be patient with people? We do. Why should we be kind in this doggy-dog world? We should be kind, because God is kind to us. Why should we keep forgiving people?

God is a forgiving God. He forgives us when we repent and confess our sins.

Use your reflective journal to measure your own spiritual temperature. Write about a time when you could have used more patience. Take some time to think about times when God was patient with you. Give thanks to the Lord.

Name three things in your life that you are passionate about. Jesus is so passionate about us that He died for us, went to hell and rose on the third day.

_____

_____

_____

_____

_____

_____

_____

Chapter 10

Get a Vision for Success

Write the vision and make it plain is a Biblical principle that can help us to keep the plan God reveals before us. Have you noticed that when you write something down, you tend to remember the details better? You don't lose sight or focus as easily and you can share the ideas quickly with others. In this portion of the book, we are going to do what is called *vision casting*. We are going to spend some time looking at where we want to go.

The way we see ourselves is so important in how others will see us. We have to believe and receive the truth about whom we are and where we are headed in life. I encountered a lot of bullies growing up in New York City. I believe bullies can be found anywhere and in any race, age and or culture. Looking back, I realize that I attracted some of the bullies in my life because of the way I saw myself. I saw myself as small, insignificant and weak. I was a little girl in a big city with big schools. My parents moved around a lot and this impacted my social ability. I became an introvert, who feared rejection. The children in the school yard didn't know all this. They simply saw a shy, awkward girl, who was an easy target for their jokes and abuse. I grew up and moved to another city, but I carried the baggage of the *little me-big you mentality*. The bullies found me. There was always an awkward situation or conversation at my expense, because I hadn't dealt with the fear of rejection.

Once I understood this about myself (much later in life), I was able to pray against the spirit of fear and make choices to go out of my comfort zone. I started to journal about the people places and things that impacted my life, so that I could reflect later. Now, I have broken free. The little girl who couldn't stand in front of her class when called on and the young woman who couldn't stand up for herself at work, has become someone who loves to try new things, meet new people and explore new territory. No matter what God tells you to do in your life, you simply need to work as unto the Lord and thank God for His grace and mercy. He will sometimes allow us to walk into difficult situations, but He will never leave nor forsake us.

I didn't see my potential. I saw my limitations. I focused on the fact that I struggled with math and that I was always the last child picked in gym class. I continued to feel shy and awkward. I ran into the same situation at every new school. It made me feel unlovable. I'm sure that someone can relate to what happed to me. You may have had the spirit of fear or you may have had a bully mentality or both. Just being honest with yourself and knowing who you are, is the first step to making positive changes in your life. The enemy comes into our lives to steal kill and destroy, but remember, we have the victory through what Jesus did for us on Calvary. Instead of focusing on your weaknesses, try focusing on your strengths. You can become great at whatever you are called to do!

Each person that is born into the world is born with only one possession, their life. We are free to believe anyway we see fit. This is called free will. Social norms try to dictate what is acceptable in any given region we are born in, but whether we choose to conform to those norms is totally up to us. Most people conform to whatever social norms they are brought up in, but some rebel. God has made every human being an offer that shouldn't be refused. He has given us the offer of Salvation through the Blood of Jesus. Our lives are so precious to God that He secured an eternal spot in Heaven for each of us who believes in the sinless Blood of Jesus. Think about that truth for a moment. Jesus said,

"In My Father's House are many mansions: if *it were* not *so*, I would have told you. I go to prepare a place for you." John 14:2 NKJ

This isn't a fairytale. This is a spiritual fact. God has mansions in Heaven for all His children. He is a kind, loving Father who provides in Heaven and on earth. Why would anyone deny themselves the opportunity to get to know Him? One reason some people deny God, is because of a false sense of what a father is. God is not a grumpy old man in the sky waiting to throw you into hell for every mistake. Instead, He is a loving, compassionate Father extending forgiveness, grace and mercy. Don't abuse grace and rape mercy, it won't work out in your favor.

God is not mocked that what a man sows he will also reap. KJV

Jesus was tempted at every point, yet lived a sinless life. He can relate to what we go through and will intercede on our behalf. God wants you to take the time to get to know Him so that He can show you wonderful things that you never knew. Perfect love cast out fear. The love of God makes the righteous bold as a lion. Be bold in your faith.

What you do, don't do and allow in your life are products of what you meditate on and what you say. It started as a thought and turned into an action. Somewhere along the way, it is almost certain that you spoke of it. Our thoughts come from our influences. Meditate on the Word to receive the original, pure thoughts that God intended for you. When Satan interjects a negative thought, cast it down.

Casting down imaginations, and every high thing that exalts itself against the knowledge of God, and bringing into captivity every thought to the obedience of Christ. 2 Corinthians 10:5 KJV

This is important to your spiritual and mental health. "You only live once," is a saying that is common in the United States. We live here on earth once, but our souls will wake up to live again in Heaven or hell, throughout eternity. The choice is ours. God makes it clear in His Word that He has set before us life or death, blessing or cursing. He wants us to choose life. God created us because of His desire to have a family. God is a loving Father to all that will come to Him.

How do you get a vision for your life? You've already begun the process. This process includes getting to know God as father, getting to know yourself and starting to write in your journal. Write the vision make it plain, so that those who read it will run.

Your vision is unique and personal to your experience. Everyone is different in their hopes, dreams and desires. Dr. Myles Monroe was quoted as saying, *"Sight is a function of the eyes, but vision is a function of the heart."* These words ring true to my spirit. Allow God to download His vision into your spirit and you will know in your heart what you are to do with your life. Your God-given desires will come to pass when you surrender your life to Him, through Jesus by the power of the Holy Spirit.

When you have spent some time with the Lord in prayer, He will reveal things about your life and your future. Most people pray to God for things and circumstances. Make sure *thanking Him and praising Him* for who He is a part of your prayer life. Take the time to listen to what God says back to you. He can speak to you like no one can and then, take the time to write it down. Anything God imparts to you is worth taking note of. You will soon learn that reflecting on your notes will bring you to a place of deeper revelation.

Once you've started this part of the journaling process, you will be able to determine a *vision for your life*. God has a purpose for each person on the planet. Many live their whole lives pursuing things like the American dream, political power, prestige, sexual fulfillment, fame and fortune, only to find that these things bring little, to no fulfillment. The only way to live a thrilling and fulfilling life is to surrender that life to the Lord. When you do this, you are trusting the Creator of Heaven and earth with your destiny. God is omniscient, omnipresent and omnipotent. He will never fail!

Since the age of seven, I've enjoyed creative writing. Being a shy little girl, creative writing gave me a chance to communicate my ideas. This isn't the case for everyone. I realize there are many individuals that are analytical and enjoy things like science and math more than reading and writing. There are also extroverts, who love to talk much more than write. The good thing about journaling is that it can be done at your own pace, in your own way. I just provide a guideline to assist you in the process.

Journaling for success is different from writing in a diary. Journaling for success is purposeful. Your first objective is to define your goals by getting to know yourself better. As you get to know yourself better, you'll be able to have a better sense of direction and purpose for your life. Many people have fallen away from freehand writing. Many use a computer to type out their thoughts. That is fine, because the way you journal isn't as important as journaling itself. If you can freehand, I think it brings a more personal touch to the experience.

As we learn to write down our thoughts and connect our hopes and dreams with the promises of God, we will notice a change in our hearts. When we read the Word of God, it penetrates our hearts and when we write the vision, it reinforces what we've learned. It is also a testimony later to others of what God is doing in you and through you. Let not mercy and truth forsake thee: bind them about thy neck; write them upon the table of thine heart. Prov. 3:3

Do you hate writing? Try journaling, using the format outlined in this book for about 30 days, and see how beneficial it is to you. If you find it difficult to write out your thoughts, try using an *audio recorder*. The idea is to have a record to reflect on later. You'll be surprised to see how you progress and how being able to bring things back to your memory, will help your perspective of where you are emotionally, physically and spiritually.

Spend some time in prayer and write down some things that come to mind for the vision for your life. Remember to enter into prayer with a thankful attitude and a grateful heart. Add three things to your journal that you are thankful for.

_____

_____

_____

_____

_____

Chapter 11

Habit Forming

It's been determined that it takes about 30 days to form a habit. Before you journal about some habits you'd like to form, start with the habits you need to break. I have a confession. I was once addicted to chocolate. I jokingly called myself a chocoholic. I ate it almost every day. I would swing by the dollar store and buy packs of the delicious treat. I would hide the packages from my family, because I didn't want to share. The weight crept up on me, but I didn't care enough to stop eating chocolate on an almost daily basis. I'll answer a question that is probably going through the minds of many readers. Do I still eat chocolate every day? The answer is no. I still enjoy chocolate, but not daily. I replaced chocolate with healthier treats.

I came to the conclusion that I was an emotional eater. I made a conscious decision to stop living to eat and start *eating to live*. I feel so much better and I lost some weight with God's help. My point is, simply, that we sometimes have to determine what our problem behaviors are before we can determine what positive habit will be most effective.

I remember the first time I became aware of the need to renew the mind. I was a brand new believer sitting in a little church in the country. I was so excited to be there. I was what some would call, a baby Christian and on fire for God! I had a made-up mind. I knew Jesus was Lord and I was going to serve Him all the days of my life. I still feel this way.

The Word of God states, And be not conformed to this world: but be ye transformed by the renewing of your mind, that ye may prove what *is* the good, and acceptable, and perfect, will of God. Romans 12:2 KJV

When I heard the preacher say it was important to renew your mind, I felt some sort of conviction come over me. It was just a gentle nudge from the Holy Spirit that this was something I needed to do. How would I do this? What were the steps? Where would I sign up to get this done? It took some time, but through studying and much prayer, I came to the understanding that a renewed mind is a continual process that the believer undergoes, while replacing old mindsets and opinions with the truth of God's Word.

Webster defines the word, renew, as to make like new, to restore freshness. To refresh, means to give new life or brightness. To restore, means bring back to a former state to recondition and to renovate. My old way of looking at it, was to restore something to good condition or to revive and refresh one's spirit. I now realize that God makes all things brand new. I don't have a refurbished mind. I have a new mind in Christ. The Bible also tells us that it's not good to put new wine into old wine skins, because they would burst. I hope this brings clarity about the mind renewal process.

Don't let Satan in your life with wrong thinking. You become what you believe. Negative thoughts may come, but we are told to cast down evil imaginations and to meditate on things that are pure, lovely and good report. When negative thoughts try to come into our mind, purposely think of a scripture reference. Change the channel. Casting down imaginations that exalt themselves above the knowledge of God, is important for spiritual and mental health.

A part of my struggle was always seeing my glass as half empty. I guess, I was a bit of a pessimist. I had let the pressures of life weigh me down, to the point of lost hope. The Bible says that hope deferred makes the heart sick. You can become very pessimistic, when you lose hope. The key is to never let your hope die. God is able to do exceedingly abundantly above all that we could ever ask or think. Don't be discouraged, if things don't happen in your way or on your timetable. Surrender your will to the perfect Will of God.

Some people resist God, because they are ashamed of or attached to their sinful ways. God is not looking for perfect people. He wants us to come to Him just as we are. We are to strive for perfection, which means maturity in the things of God. We are like sheep, because sheep are vulnerable without a shepherd. We need a shepherd. Jesus is the Good Shepherd. Don't get man-made traditions mixed up with the commands of God. Religion is not relationship. Relationship is your personal communication with God. How much time is required in your prayer life? Talk to God and He will lead you into a Holy Ghost session. I can say from my personal experience that daily speaking in other tongues, quiet time to just listen and reading the Bible are very important.

My journaling time has also helped me expound on the truths God has revealed to me. Agree with the great plan God has for your life. One key to receiving God's best, is simply being obedient to His Will. When we try to override God with what we think, it never works. God has seen the end from the beginning. He knows all about you, your circumstance and your future and yes, He still loves you. God has the perfect perspective, because He sees the past, present and future.

There is a parable in the Bible, where a father asked his eldest son to go work in the fields. One son said no, but eventually obeyed his father and went. His other son said, "Yes father, I will go but never did." Who obeyed their father? It was the one who actually did what the father asked. (Paraphrase Matthew 21:28-32)

God requires obedience, not lip service. I am a firm believer that nothing is impossible with God. God will not force His will in our lives, but He does reveal His will to us. It's up to us to obey. God hates sin, but He loves the sinner. God so loved the world that He gave His only begotten Son, so that whoever would believe in Him shall be saved. John 3:16 KJV

That's called the good news of the Gospel. In order to truly renew your mind, it would be a good idea to understand what behaviors God likes and dislikes in a person. These examples can be found, throughout the Bible. Let's start with developing an understating of what God does not like:

Proverbs 6 verses 16-19 sum it up well in saying, these six things doth the LORD hate: yea, seven are an abomination unto him. A proud look, a lying tongue, and hands that shed innocent blood, a heart that devises wicked imaginations, feet that be swift in running to mischief, false witness that speak lies, and he that sows discord among brethren. KJV

I always wondered why these verses of scripture were written this way. There are clearly seven items, but it starts by saying six things the Lord hates, yea seven are an abomination. As I studied, I learned that this is a poetic form of writing that would correspond with a countdown in today's language. For example, a D.J. would give the top ten countdown holding on to the number one song until the end, emphasizing it as the most popular song. When we examine our own hearts, as the Bible tells us to do, we should be especially mindful to guard our heart against any of these evil things that can creep in.

The Bible gives us real accounts of real people, who struggled with these issues. Jesus was the only sinless person, making Him the ultimate example of what *to do*. He said to His disciples, "Follow me." Jesus will always lead us in the right direction. God loves the world, but hates the world's system.

Allow God to work on you from the inside out. A renovation can look like a disaster zone to most people, but God sees the end from the beginning. Man looks at the outward appearance, but God looks at and searches the heart of man. Don't count people out, because God isn't finished with any of us yet.

Today, I have renewed my mind to the truth that I can do all things through Christ who strengthens me and like you God has a specific plan for my life. This revelation came to me as a result of studying the Word of God. I have to say that it was a process for me to believe that a woman who grew up poor in New York City, who was known as the shy awkward kid most of my school years, who grew up to have failed marriages, financial troubles, dropped out of college twice, before earning a Bachelor's degree in psychology and was diagnosed with a chemical imbalance in my brain, could do *all things through Christ*. I found out that the key to doing *all things* is ***through Christ***.

God has given His children power from on High. Receive it and walk in it. God's Word also tells us that we can overcome obstacles put in our path through the Blood of the Lamb and the Word of our testimony. The power is through a life sold out to God. Embrace this truth and the truth will set you free from any bondage in your life

The way we see ourselves can affect the way we see others. Remember, there is no big I and little you in the Kingdom of God. We are all His beloved. Having a negative self-image may make you feel like you're not worthy of success. This type of thinking can hinder you from doing wonderful and exciting things to enrich your life and the lives of others. We are all fearfully and wonderfully made in the Image of God. He wants you to know how loved you are through a personal relationship with Him. When you seek Him, you will find Him when you search with all your heart.

Behold, I stand at the door, and knock: if any man hears my voice, and open the door, I will come in to him, and will sup with him, and he with Me. Revelation 3:20 KJV

There are also people who see themselves as superior to others. The scriptures reveal to us;

For I say, through the grace given unto me, to every man that is among you, not to think *of himself* more highly than he ought to think; but to think soberly, according as God hath dealt to every man the measure of faith. KJV

When we get a revelation of God's love, we begin to see the *value in every human soul*. God created us, because He wanted a family. We are all precious in His sight. If someone falls short, we are to pray for them. Our love and acceptance of others shouldn't be based on anything, except the command of God, which is to love your neighbor as yourself.

When I became a new Christian, I would enjoy listening to preachers but I would only read my Bible on occasion. As I later learned, this was an immature, carnal approach at Bible study. I was convicted about this behavior. I grew, when I started spending quality time in the Word of God. Now, I have read the Bible through in its entirety several times and I love doing it. Spending time in the Word of God is very fulfilling. I learn something new every time. I also study the Bible by looking up specific topics and applying the principles to my life. It really works when *you work it*.

When you acknowledge a bad habit, it becomes easier to overcome that bad habit. Go on to the next habit on your list. Denial keeps us in bondage to whatever the real problem is. Get to the root of your problems, by being honest with yourself. Forming a good habit should then be implemented. For example, if you want to build better study habits, create an environment conducive for studying. Set a time of day aside. God loves the first fruits of our day. Turn off the television and anything that may interrupt you. Organize your study area.

Breaking a bad habit, like emotional eating, can be more difficult. Start by once again acknowledging the bad habit. Determine the triggers that cause you to over indulge in the behavior, then find a healthier way to reward your good behavior as you transition. It may take time, but willful, repetitively behavior changes can become a lifestyle change.

There are occasions when a doctor should be consulted. Some cravings are the way the human body makes you aware of deficiencies. Talk to your doctor about major struggles.

When trying to make or break any habit, be aware that it does take time. Don't feel defeated if you stumble in the beginning. Just pick up where you left off in the process. You'll discover that the 30-day rule really does work. It won't be long before your mindset changes about the matter. *Victory is in sight*. You can be free from any addiction, bad behavior, struggle or wrong mindset. The Blood of Jesus has set us free. We can do all things through Christ who strengthens us. We know this because the Word of God tells us we have the mind of Christ. As we grow up in a world full of crime, rage, violence, depression, confusion, lies and selfish ambition, we can become infected. We are in this world, but not of this world. Accept the fact that Jesus has provided healing for every area of your life. There is nothing missing and nothing lacking in Christ.

The only way to stay above the cares of this world is to be filled with the Holy Spirit on a daily basis. This is done by spending time in prayer, meditation and studying God's Word. The choice is yours to make. You can be filled with the things of this world or be filled with the power of the Holy Spirit. Which do you choose? Be encouraged in your journey. No matter what stage of life you are in, remember, *God has a way of making all things new.*

Think about your habits, thoughts, mindsets and behaviors. What recent improvements have you made in your life? As you get to know yourself, you'll be able to assess behaviors, patterns and habits that you want to change or you may discover things you want to enhance.

_____

_____

_____

_____

_____

_____

_____

_____

_____

_____

Chapter 12

Build a Bridge to Your Success

Are you ready to dig deep within yourself? Ask yourself where you're headed in life. Hopefully, you're going in the right direction. It helps to do a self-check from time to time. When you identify what your life boosters are and what your life drainers are, you will be able to take authority in those areas.

The years of my life that I spoke negatively about myself on a regular basis did damage. I would look at myself and criticize my looks, my personality and my intelligence. Unfortunately, I learned the hard way that you will have what you say and that, as a man speaks so is he. I started to age fast. I considered myself shy and awkward, so I didn't maintain healthy relationships and when I returned to college, I struggled. By the time it finally sank in that I could help myself by what I said, I was already in a mess. I was diagnosed with a chemical imbalance in my brain. I almost sank into the quicksand of mental health issues until God stepped in.

I used my faith and believed what my dedicated pastors taught us on divine health and faith. I began to speak and believe that I was healed. God did such a quick work in my life. It may seem like it took a long time to some, but God was right on time. God inspired me to share this aspect of my life as an encouragement to others. There is no name greater than the *Name of Jesus*. Yes, Jesus healed me. God is so good! Today, we need to understand the power of words and names. We need to embrace the idea that we have a certain measure of creative power just by what we say. For example, if we are diagnosed with an illness, we can do one of two things.

We can agree with the illness, talk about the illness and prepare to die or we can take authority over the illness by speaking life and, of course, following sound medical advice. *God is a healer*. When we feed our spirit the life-giving food which is the Word of God, it stirs up our faith. Learn the Will of God by studying His Word and speak the Will of God to see it come to pass in your life.

Write the Will of God in your journal. Search out His promises in the Bible. Believe them, receive them and write them down as a daily reminder.

Here are a few promises from the Word of God to get you started.

And all these blessings shall come on thee, and overtake thee, if thou shalt hearken unto the voice of the Lord thy God. Deuteronomy 28:2

Train up a child in the way he should go: and when he is old, he will not depart from it Proverbs 22:6 KJV

Children, obey your parents in the Lord: for this is right. Honor thy father and mother; which is the first commandment with promise; that it may be well with thee, and thou may live long on the earth.

And, ye fathers provoke not your children to wrath: but bring them up in the nurture and admonition of the Lord. Ephesians 6:1-4

But in every nation he that fears Him, and works righteousness, is accepted with Him. Acts 10:35

For whom the Lord loves, He corrects, even as a father, the son in whom he delights. Proverbs 3:12

And ye are complete in Him, which is the head of all principality and power: Colossians 2:10

A man shall be satisfied with good by the fruit of his mouth: and the recompense of a man's hands shall be rendered unto him. Proverbs 12:14

Whatsoever thy hand finds to do, do it with thy might; for there is no work, nor device, nor knowledge, nor wisdom, in the grave, whither thou go. Ecclesiastes 9:10

Have you ever considered that speaking life over someone, who may have offended you, may change your perspective of them? Say what God says about people. Let positive words take root in their lives and yours. Life and death are in the power of the tongue. We basically have what we say. Look around you. Do you like what you see? If not, consider what is coming out of your mouth.

Natural Facts	Spiritual Truths
Illness	*Divine Health*
Poverty	*Prosperity*
Death	*Eternal Life*

When we renew our minds, we put in thoughts of hope, love, joy, prosperity, peace sanctification, holiness, righteousness, salvation, patience, goodness, faith, victory, boldness, success and mercy. This is not just for us, but it is a blessing to others. Take out strife, hate, bitterness, anger, envy, jealousy, gossip, wrath, vengeance, fear, lust, depression, guilt, pride, greed, doubt, and condemnation.

I've had the privilege of interviewing many successful people. The thing they had most in common was their outlook on life. They were all positive people, who had a vision and weren't shy about pursuing it. They were also disciplined. Success comes when the right balance is applied to your life.

One major key to success is being humble enough to recognize that you need God in your life.

Humble yourself in the sight of the Lord and He will exalt you in due season. KJV

Everyone has a different definition of success. My personal definition is spiritual growth and victory over depression. Your personal success story doesn't have to mimic anyone else's. God won't twist your arm, but in the end you lose, when you don't obey God. We can't just emulate what successful people are doing. That doesn't work all the time, and if it works at all, it could be short lived. *We have to do what God tells us to do.* We can only do what He tells us do when we know His voice. He explains that His sheep know His voice and another they will not follow. We need a personal revelation. Let's get a clear picture of what hearing God's voice would look like. God used Moses to deliver His people from under the harsh rule of Pharaoh.

They got to the Red Sea and faith caused the Red Sea to part for Moses and God's people. When Pharaoh and his army pursued them, they saw Moses and the Israelites passing through on dry land. They assumed that because Moses was successful at crossing over on dry land, that they could pursue and overtake them. Instead Pharaoh and his army drowned, because God did not tell them to follow. Our motives and intents have a lot to do with our success.

Be not deceived; God is not mocked. Whatsoever a man sows, that shall he also reap. Galatians 6:7

This is an important principle to comprehend. You can't step on people to get to the top, you can't sleep your way to the top and you can't do absolutely nothing and expect a miracle. You have to walk by faith, trusting and obeying God's Word for yourself. If you were asked for your official statement on life, you can now give a spiritual truth instead of a natural fact.

You can choose life or death, blessings or curses. God desires for you to choose life and live throughout eternity ruling and reigning with Him.

What obstacles are hindering your progress in life?

Take an honest self-assessment and see if you need to purge anything from your lifestyle. Write about it.

_____

_____

_____

_____

_____

_____

_____

_____

_____

_____

_____

_____

Chapter 13

Use Your Authority

In the book of Genesis, it is clear that God used His words to create the Universe and everything in it. He gave us a version of this creative power. For example, when God said, "let there be light." There was light. Gen 1:3

When we say things about ourselves that line up with the promises found in God's Word, we facilitate those things coming to pass in our lives. We must not only speak the Word, but obey the Word as well.

Let's take another look at names. When a name was given in Biblical days, it represented what the person was. Every day, that person was called that name, thus people spoke that thing over them. Today, many people put little thought in the meaning of the names they give their children.

Parents don't always take into consideration the fact that their child will be called this name every day of their life. There is power in what we say and do. No matter what name you were given, you can still walk in the blessings of God by believing and confessing the promises of God over your life. When we speak life over ourselves, we facilitate an environment where good things can happen. When we speak negativity, we create an environment for negative things to happen. However, we should understand the important fact that we are not all powerful. Bad things can still happen to good people. Stay encouraged. We are overcomers in Christ!

We reap what we sow. Even though we live in a dispensation of Grace, it doesn't mean we won't reap a negative thing. It just means we have time to repent and change. To repent means to turn away from the sin. Many people have trouble admitting that there is sin in their life. If you have an issue with sin, the only way to be free is to repent and confess it.

If we confess our sins, he is faithful and just to forgive us our sins, and to cleanse us from all unrighteousness. 1John 1:9 KJV

When we *speak life,* we frame our world into what it should be. We should speak the Word of God daily to avoid problems, but if a problem comes our way, we can overcome it by the Blood of the Lamb and the Word of our testimony. If you have a problem, the best thing to do is to understand that Jesus is the solution. Find a scriptural promise and stand on it. Speak those things that be, not as though they were.

We have to learn to use our God given authority to rise above whatever comes our way. We can't use our God given authority, if we don't know or believe that we have it. The Bible illustrates that to us when it mentions the fact that a child, who is heir to a fortune is like a slave until he grows up and is able to manage his affairs on his own. As long as you don't realize the power God has given you, you are like a baby in a golden crib. That child may be heir to a fortune, but until he matures and becomes aware of his authority, he doesn't make any decisions to benefit himself. When you grow up in the things of God and accept his plan for your life, you become able to enjoy the benefits of being mature in the Lord.

God wants you to live a prosperous life. When I looked up the word prosperity, it was defined as; success, affluence, wealth, opulence, luxury, ease, plenty, comfort and well-being. This definition is nice, but let me go on the record as saying that prosperity in God is all that and more. It is wholeness, freedom, love, joy, peace in the mist of life's storms and eternal life. Prosperity God's way will equal intimacy with Him which covers you in every way.

Let's recap. You're getting to know God and yourself and you have a vision of a prosperous future. You have determined what habits you want to break and what habits you want to create. Now, let's *build that bridge* to your successful outcome. God says He knows the plans He has for you. He talks about giving you hope and an expected end. Because God knows the direction you should go, you must trust and rely on Him in all things.

God has healed, delivered and set us free. We just have to receive it. Only God can take your mess and make it your message and your test and make it your testimony. Surrender to the one, true, living God who loves you so much. God has promised to save us and forgive us of all our sins. Forgiveness is a big deal to God. It's so important, that we are required to forgive those that trespass against us. Forgiveness is therapeutic to the forgiver and the forgiven. When we choose to hold a grudge, it only creates bitterness and strife.

Think for a moment about if God had not forgiven us through the Blood of Jesus. Hope would be lost. The good news is that we can not only be forgiven, but we can be made new.

Let's continue building your bridge to success. Pull out your journal. Start by listing three areas of your life that you would like to see improved upon within the next 30 days. These will be your short term goals. We will get into your long term goals later. Take time to really think about what works for you and what needs to change. Some people want to lose weight. Some people want to make friends and some just want to get their home and/or office organized. No matter what it is, with God's help, we are going to build a bridge to reach your personal goals.

For example, if you need a financial breakthrough, find several scriptures on prosperity. Write them down. Make a daily confession and most importantly, make a lifestyle change to match what the Word is speaking on.

Tithing and giving seem like foolishness to the world, but I, like many others have seen God's hand in my life time and time again, because I freely tithe and give. Bring ye all the tithes into the storehouse, that there may be meat in Mine house, and prove Me now herewith, says the Lord of Hosts, if I will not open you the windows of Heaven, and pour you out a blessing, that there shall not be room enough to receive it. Malachi 3:10 KJV

Obeying this Biblical principle will result in blessings. There is no greater position than to be a child of God. True prosperity begins when sin is washed off your life with the Blood of Jesus.

After my husband of seven years committed suicide, I was left without any money in savings. He had given some of our personal belongings away to his friends. I felt like a broken, depressed widow, who was literally down to my last $65. (I had to remember the fact that my Father owns the cattle on a thousand hills.) The Lord spoke to my heart and told me to buy the First Lady of the church, scripture. I wondered why the Lord was asking me to do that. She was the First Lady. I'm sure she had Bibles and things with scripture references. Her birthday was coming up and I would have preferred to give her jewelry, because I wanted to impress her, not offend her. Nevertheless, I was obedient. I found this beautifully framed scripture of Proverbs 31, describing the Virtuous Woman. The price came to about $65, when the tax was included. Wow, what a day! I really wanted to get her a bracelet for $29.99 and keep the change, but I was **obedient** to what the Lord said. Well, the very next day, I received a checkbook in the mail for a money market account in my name for $65,000. I was shocked, because I had fought with my deceased husband's insurance company to receive a $30,000 insurance policy from his death. Because he failed to reveal he was a smoker and committed suicide, I was told several times that I would receive nothing.

I called the insurance company to make sure they had not made a mistake. The gentleman on the line stated they had not sent me a check. I explained that I was not holding a check, but a checkbook for a money market account which was double the amount of the insurance policy. After some frustrated checking on his part, he stated "Lady just keep it!" I knew this was from God. My obedience opened a window of opportunity to pour out His blessings upon me. God is no respecter of persons. I hate to admit that along my journey, there have been times that I missed blessings out of disobedience. Our simple acts of obedience set us up to be blessed, in every area of our lives. There have been other times in my life where money was given to me from an unexpected source.

There have also been times where I was used to be a financial blessing. As a believer, we must see money as a tool. We must be able to believe God for what is needed and also to release what is needed to advance the Kingdom of

God. When you have gone from the contemplation stage to the implementation stage that's when things start to happen. What are you waiting for? I'm sure that like most people, you've tried relying on your own strength and other people, only to be grossly disappointed. Put your trust in God. That is when the best part of life begins.

So far, we've discussed the importance of positive self-talk, habit breaking and forming and obedience. It's so important to speak life over oneself and to obey God. God did the work for us. We just have to agree with what He says about us. His Word is filled with promises for every aspect of life. Use your creative power to bring positive things into your life. Having the right perspective is the first step. You can build a bridge to success by speaking the promises of God, researching Biblical promises and writing a promise a day in your journal.

Take some time to journal about your priorities. List the five most important things in your life today. Find Biblical promises associated with what you want. Speak the promises out loud throughout your day.

_____

_____

_____

_____

_____

_____

_____

_____

_____

_____

_____

_____

Chapter 14

Reinforce Your Bridge

It's not fruitful to discover the right thing to do, but only do it once or twice or worse, not to do it at all. Once we discover the right thing to do, we need to make that our way of life. Years ago, I joined a gym. I was so excited about the idea of getting in shape. After only a few visits, I got distracted and never returned. I didn't understand the value of what I was doing for myself. If I had, I would have continued. Today, I enjoy taking walks to stay heart healthy.

A self-sabotaging trap that many people fall into is lack of consistency. Everyone is excited about the newest fad, until it becomes common knowledge. Start searching for things that are more than fads in your life. Find things that work for you and make it a lifestyle.

Healthy livings should be a priority in life. You only get one Earth suit. Take care of it. Our bodies are the temple of the Holy Spirit. The Bible tells us that the Holy Spirit lives within us. Take care of yourself. You can start by feeding your body healthy foods and feeding your spirit the Word of God. You can talk to your doctor about an exercise regimen. You can exercise your mind by reading. Many people detox their bodies with lemon and water. You can also detox your soul by guarding what you watch and listen to. Get plenty of sleep and be happy on purpose. Work with divine health, not against it.

I never liked diets, because I couldn't stick with most of them. When I found a healthy way of looking at food, I changed my habits and the way I thought about food and made it a lifestyle. You can do this too. No matter what it is in your life that needs to change, you can apply the principles of identifying the problem, working on a goal to resolve the problem and implementing the plan of action for results.

Mind	Body	Spirit
Reading	*Walking*	*Bible Study*
Journaling	*Swimming*	*Bible Memorization*
Taking classes	*Cycling*	*Meditation*
Relaxation Techniques	*Pilates*	*Church Participation*
Socializing	*Diet*	*Reciting Bible Promises*

After you have the green light from your doctor, look into your local gym memberships, healthy eating plans, support groups for whatever may be a factor in your life and of course the Word of God. The Bible was written with you in mind. We can uncover truth about every area of our life, even how to live a healthier lifestyle. The treasures are there to be dug out by serious believers. Many local churches offer free nutrition and/or exercise classes. When you feel your best, you look your best. I'm working toward being the best version of me that I can be. I can't be you and you can't be me. We can walk out our life journey pursuing all that God has called us to be. We can be whole in mind, body and spirit. Life is a precious gift. We can enjoy life, when we learn to appreciate who we are and who we belong to.

As children of God and heir's to the promises of God, it is our duty to know these promises. Once we are educated on what Bible says we can have, we can equip ourselves by standing on the promises we have learned. Here is a great place to start. And it shall come to pass, if thou shalt hearken diligently unto the voice of the Lord thy God, to observe and to do all His commandments which I commanded thee this day, that the Lord thy God will set thee on high above all the nations. And all these blessings shall come on thee, and overtake thee, if thou shalt hearken unto the voice of the Lord thy God. Deut. 28:1-2 KJV

When we equip ourselves and apply the Word of God to our lives, we find a supernatural strength. Don't struggle with life-purpose questions. Get busy for God and you will find purpose and fulfillment. Once you become a member of a Bible preaching church, you should then find some way to get involved with Kingdom business.

One way to put oneself in a position of power is to boldly confess the Promises. I can't reiterate this principle enough. Talk to your circumstances and tell them what you want to happen. It's a process. It may take some time. Faith comes by hearing and hearing by the Word of God. Jesus once walked up to a fig tree in a time when there should have been ripe figs on the tree. Jesus saw that the tree was barren, cursed the fig tree and it withered soon after. The disciples marveled at how soon the fig tree withered. Jesus told them that if they just had faith they could speak with the same power. Faith is a powerful gift from God.

Jesus said to His disciples, "Verily I say unto you, if ye have faith, and doubt not, ye shall not only do this, which is done to the fig tree, but also if ye shall say unto this mountain, be thou removed, and be thou cast into the sea, it shall be done." Matthew 21:21 KJV

The Apostle Paul was a powerful evangelist and one of the greatest contributors to the Bible.

He found a passion and zeal for the spreading the Word of God and he was committed to it even unto death. Paul started out as a passionate man who believed he was standing for what was right. He passionately sought to punish and kill the followers of Jesus Christ. He did this, because he was led to believe that they were blasphemers and trouble makers. In the Bible, Stephen was stoned for his faith. The witnesses laid their coats at the feet of a young man named Saul, who would go onto to persecute Christians, until he was converted on the road of Damascus and became the Apostle Paul.

So many people are like Paul. They have a false impression of who Christ is, because of people who have misrepresented Jesus. Jesus is Love. He gave His life for each and every one of us to have the opportunity to rule and reign with Him. Paul was on his way to prosecute Christians in a town called Damascus, when he had a personal encounter with Jesus.

This encounter changed his life. He made a lifestyle change. Instead of pursuing Christians to destroy them, he became one of them and pursued spreading the Gospel with passion, courage, dedication and conviction.

One thing that every person on the planet will be accountable for is their own belief. We will all stand before God and answer for what we did and said and why we did it. If we reject Jesus, the Son of God, we will be rejected to enter into eternal life. Make sure that your opinions of Jesus aren't based on the opinions of man. Seek the Lord for yourself while He may be found. There is a small timeframe of opportunity available to you. Take it.

Journaling about your eating habits may reveal truths that help you with weight loss or weight gain goals.

In your Journal, create a list of healthy activities. Circle the ones you engage in on a regular basis. Underline the ones you would like to add to your healthy lifestyle routine. Write about some life changes that would make you healthier.

_____

_____

_____

_____

_____

_____

_____

_____

_____

_____

_____

_____

Chapter 15

Start Moving Forward

Everyone wants to advance in life. It's hard to find one person on this planet that would say, "I don't want to go forward. I don't want to do better. I want to go backward. I like being stuck where I am." Now, I'm aware that there are phobias that cause some people to fall back when they should press forward. There is no Name higher than the Name of Jesus. Phobias can be overcome.

For the sake of this argument, let's address healthy, productive citizens in this scenario. Even though we want to excel in life, we already determined just a few things that can slow us down or stop us all together. They are; self-defeating talk, self-defeating thoughts and behaviors, disobedience to God's Word, lack of understanding of God's Word and an unforgiving spirit. These are all things we have control over.

God gave us the ability to make a choice to change. Satan has already been defeated. If left ignored, these things will stop you from reaching your goals and fulfilling your God given destiny.

There will come a time when we all will stand before God and make an account for every idle word spoken. Accountability is so important. We have to hold ourselves accountable for our actions. We can't blame things like how we were raised, society, life pressures, influences, etc., on how we choose to live today. God created us to be social creatures. We should always seek His will by going directly to Him in prayer. He understands our desire to communicate and converse. It is a good thing to seek wise counsel. Where no counsel is, the people fall: but in the multitude of counselors there is safety. Proverbs 11:14

Every person should have someone that they can talk to. Keep in mind that the ultimate decision for your life falls on you. God will not hold your friends accountable for your choices. Be a real friend to your friends. My personal experience has been that sharing some things can be a blessing to you and the hearer, but you don't have to share everything with everybody. Be led by the Spirit. There is a time and place to share your hopes and dreams. There is also a time and place to share your victories. Unfortunately, everyone in life won't be for you. Don't surround yourself with negative people. There may be only one person in your life that you can count on. It doesn't matter how many you have, just have one and be one. A friend loves at all times, and a brother is born for adversity. Prov. 17:17

Joseph was a young man who lived in biblical times. God gave him a series of dreams of which he shared with his brethren. The dreams revealed a plan for God to favor him and use him. His brethren were already jealous of the favor and attention he received from his father, Jacob. One day, after hearing that they would one day bow down to their brother Joseph, his brothers decided to kill him. Instead, they eventually decided to sell Joseph into slavery to avoid blood being on their hands. They didn't realize that God would use the situation and raise Joseph up amongst his captures. And it came to pass, when Joseph was come unto his brethren, they stripped Joseph out of his coat, his coat of many colors that was on him; and they took him and cast him into a pit: and the pit was empty, there was no water in it. Genesis 37:23-24.

After years in slavery, Joseph became second only to Pharaoh over all the land of Egypt. After a great famine had occurred, Joseph's brothers eventually had to come to Egypt to buy food. Who did they have to bow down to for help? Unrevealed to them, it was Joseph! Human beings were created to be social creatures. The Bible makes that clear when God said, "It is not good that man should be alone, I will make him a helpmate suitable for him." Isolation can cause dysfunction. Through life's interactions with others, we learn how to behave, cooperate and work together. God does not need to socialize. He is complete, whole, omniscient and omnipotent all by Himself. He chooses to fellowship with us. He created us to rule and reign with Him. His desire is for believers to spend Eternity with Him.

You can talk to God about anything. God knew us before we were formed in our mother's womb. He knows what you think and why you think it. He made each one of us with our own DNA, fingerprints, personality and purpose. God's love knows no limits. He even loves people that choose to deny Him and go to hell. People who deny Jesus Christ won't feel the love of God throughout eternity, because they chose death over life. Jesus is life. God gave us all the gift of free will.

We are free to receive or reject His message. I chose life and I made up my mind that there is no other way for me to go.

I believe that if I had let an unforgiving spirit dictate my life, I wouldn't be able to sleep at night. Forgiveness releases the person that hurt you and helps you heal in the process. It's been a journey to get to the point of wholeness after a series of tragic events in my life. I'm an overcomer and so are you by the Blood of the Lamb and the Word of your testimony.

As Christians, we should realize that we are sometimes under a microscope. We, as believers should hold ourselves to a high standard of accountability. This doesn't mean that there is no room to be human. I realize my own strengths and weaknesses and I respect the fact that everyone has strengths and weaknesses. We are the only Bible some people will ever read. There are many people in the world that have been wounded by overzealous and religious people, who refuse to walk in humility and forgiveness. Some people hold grudges against all Christians, because of what one so-called Christian may have done to them. Dearly beloved, avenge not yourselves, but *rather* give place unto wrath: for it is written, "Vengeance *is* mine; I will repay," says the Lord. Romans 12:19 KJV

All we can do is express our beliefs with the same love and compassion Jesus used with us. The Holy Spirit does the rest. Some people associate the bad behavior of a few people with Jesus, not knowing that He is being grossly misrepresented.

Love works no ill to his neighbor: therefore, love is the fulfilling of the law. Romans 13:10.

Without love, we are a clanging symbol. God is love. When we love the Lord our God with all our heart and our neighbor as ourselves, it is then that we become a light to a dying world. Telling people that hell awaits everyone who does not give their life to Jesus is love. Spread the love of God. You don't have to be called into the 5-fold ministry to share the good News of the Gospel. Tell someone what Jesus has done in your life. Let your light shine bright. Peter asked

Jesus how many times he should forgive his neighbor. The answer amounted to as many times as it takes. We need to show people the same love and mercy that we want shown to us. The race is not given to the swift, but to those who endure until the very end. Compassion is an important characteristic in a believer. For with what judgment ye judge, ye shall be judged: and with what measure ye mete, it shall be measured to you again. Matthew 7:2

I've seen it more than once in my life, where people who were supposed to help people, actually hurt people, because of their lack of compassion. When we walk in love, compassion isn't far behind. Compassion doesn't mean not using tough love. Jesus gave us the best example of concern for the struggle of others. There was a woman in Biblical days who was caught in the act of adultery by the religious leaders of the day. They dragged her to Jesus and asked what should be done with her. Jesus understood that the religious leaders constantly tested Him in how He handled difficult situations of the day. They wanted to accuse Jesus of disobeying the law. Jesus used the wisdom given Him by His Heavenly Father. He told them that whoever was without sin could cast the first stone at her. Those words of wisdom convicted all the religious leaders. They left one by one, until Jesus and the woman were left alone. Jesus didn't cast a stone at her either. He could have had her stoned to death for her sins, as was the legal punishment for the crime of adultery.

Jesus didn't condemn her. He told her to go and *sin no more*. This act of mercy shows the compassion of the Heart of God. God is not looking for ways to punish you. God is looking for ways to grant you mercy. Receive His love and mercy for your life today. This doesn't give anyone a license to sin. God is Holy and requires our reverence and obedience. Journaling is just one tool to help identify and change negative patterns in your life. At this point, you should have a journal full of insightful things about who you are, your goals and dreams for the future. Take the next few days to reflect on what you've written. Make a commitment to seek God with your whole heart.

Find a person that you trust and share some of your new found insights. Talk about your testimony and some of your future goals. Ask God to lead you as to how transparent you should be. Your testimony may be the encouragement someone needs today.

_____

_____

_____

_____

_____

Chapter 16

Stay on Track

This may be the time where you start feeling the urge to fall off track. Like most things, the excitement of your journaling process maybe dwindling down. *Stay on track.* You can't see results if you don't press on. The journaling process is a process that requires time and commitment. You should be able to reflect on previous journal entries that will enlighten you about choices you've made and your destiny.

Some people are looking for a quick fix in life. Most people have a desire to feel successful and to receive acknowledgement for their accomplishments. Don't let your self-esteem be totally in what you do. Make sure you remember it's about who you are. Being a child of the Most High God is a privilege. Walk worthy.

I'm so thankful God didn't allow me to get my sense of identity from wealth or prestige. He developed my self-esteem *in Him*.

Don't stock up for yourselves things that moth and rust will destroy. The true treasure in life is spiritual. Use your gifts and talents to bring people closer to God. Things can't satisfy that inner desire deep within. This is a place where we have to surrender to God. Discover your purpose and use it to glorify God. Be an active waiter. While you're on the track to reaching your goal, be sure that you don't grow weary in the waiting season.

But they that wait upon the Lord shall renew their strength; they shall mount up with wings as eagles; they shall run, and not be weary; and they shall walk, and not faint. Isaiah 40:31 KJV

God's reward is worth waiting for. We are called the "microwave age" because technology has allowed us to experience things at really fast speed. God's timing isn't always our timing. Longsuffering is a fruit of the spirit. Sometimes we have to wait for our breakthrough. Be patience in your journey. But the fruit of the spirit is love, joy, peace, longsuffering, gentleness, goodness, faith, meekness, temperance against such there is no law. Galatians 5:22

When the storms of life come, you can quiet the storm by the power given to you as a believer. God can change things in your life when you put your trust in Him and obey. There is a story in the Bible about a time when Jesus and His disciples were on a boat. Jesus was asleep when a horrible storm developed. His disciples awakened Jesus from His sleep and asked Him if He cared that they were perishing? Jesus rebuked the storm by saying, "Peace be still." And the storm ceased. (Paraphrase Mark 4: 39 NKJV)

Let Jesus be your example. Speak to the storms of your life. Call on the Name of the Lord and trust Him to deliver you out of trouble. No one is exempt from trouble. This world is full of trouble. We can live in peace in spite of it. Learning to avoid trouble and be a solution to troublesome circumstances should be our goal. Many of us have survived difficult times and should not focus on *why* we went through it, but why we got through it. We are here for a reason and a season. Live out your purpose in life. We don't wrestle against flesh and blood, but against principalities. Let your trials cause you to rise up and help someone else. No matter what difficulties we face, we can always find someone who would benefit from our testimony or our help.

Refuse to quit. Never give up on your destiny. We are all destined to do something. Seek out your destiny, do what only you can do. I am beyond motivated to walk in all that God has for me. Consider your journaling as a safe time to be open and honest about how you feel and what you need in life to get to the next level. Be prepared to stand against adversity. Don't buckle under pressure. Make up your mind that no matter what comes your way, you will stand on the Promises of God and outlast the storm. When I go through tough times, I've learned to remember what my Heavenly Father told me. He said that I'm more than a conqueror through Christ Jesus. I'm valuable and blessed to be a blessing to others. Personal growth comes from being rooted and grounded in the Word of God.

Live a life pleasing to God. If you confess the promises; God will manifest the promises in your life. You have authority to defeat the enemies of your destiny. You have a *measure of faith* and *creative power* to speak over those things that are not according to the Word of God and watch them come to pass. The next time a problem comes your way, thank God for the solution. Praise Him in the mist of the storm. Remember to speak what you want, not what you have and watch your circumstances change. God's Word is a seed. Watch it grow as you speak His truth.

God always does His part. He requires us to use our faith to do our part. Keep your focus on the Kingdom. It's so important to keep your relationship with God a priority. Anything you put before Him, is an idol and is sin. We sometimes think of idols as statues in biblical times and wonder how could they have missed God like that? Well, today idols come in all forms, from movie stars to careers and relationships. Some people make things like their car an idol, when it becomes more important to wash it, rather than to spend time with God Almighty.

Faith produces results. If you are going through a storm or have a need, find a promise to stand on, pray, believe and receive. Always be thankful through the process. Be careful about talking about your problem too much. Spend more time professing God's goodness through your situation. *When we speak, we are speaking something into existence.*

Have you ever made a promise to someone and then, were unable or unwilling to keep that promise? I have. God is not like man. Every promise is a yes with the Lord. He doesn't struggle to keep His Word. He is the Word. In the beginning was the Word and the Word was with God and the Word was God. John 1: 1

Let God's Word heal every area of your life.

Here are just a few more promises from God's Word.

Scripture promises from: Speak the Word by Marilyn Hickey and Sarah Bowling

Psalm 32:8 "I will instruct you and teach you in the way which you should go; I will counsel you with my eye upon you."

Romans 8:11 The Spirit of Him that raised Jesus from the dead dwells in me; therefore, He that raised up Christ from the dead has quickened my mortal body, making it immune to every sickness and disease."

Ephesians 4:29 "No corrupt communication shall come out of my mouth today, for I speak words of faith and edification. Therefore, my words bring life and joy."

Write down a victory that you have had since you began your journaling process.

_____

_____

_____

_____

_____

_____

_____

_____

_____

Chapter 17

Take Someone with You

Journaling can be very beneficial to your relationships.

Make your life an open-book testimony of the goodness of God. Share the good news that Jesus is Lord. We are all called to the ministry of reconciliation. Take someone with you. Ask people if you can pray with them. Give them an invitation to know Jesus as Lord. Be kind to people as they mature in the things of God. As we have therefore opportunity, let us do good unto all men, especially unto them who are of the household of faith. Galatians 6:10.

I've encountered many people who say they believe in Heaven, but don't believe in hell. I have to tell you that this reminds me of the days of Christopher Columbus. Many didn't believe the Earth was round, but it was. It's also like not believing there is air, because you can't see it. The spiritual realm exists because the Word of God is true. Our perspective plays a big part in what type of day we have. Some see the cup half full, while others see the cup half empty. I would be the last person to pretend that tough times won't come our way, but He has given us power and authority over the forces of darkness. Don't set up camp in times of trouble. Sometimes you have to go through to *get to the other side.* I can honestly say from personal experience, that God can turn your any situation around for our good. Keep your focus on the Word, which holds the solutions to every problem you could ever face. Jesus is the answer. Let the Word of God give you your perspective.

Love unifies the body of Christ. When you walk in love, you understand that each part of the body has a different function, but that all are needed. Value your gift and the gifts in others. In the Book of Acts, the church held everything in common, including their finances. When a couple attempted to deceive the apostles and withhold some of their earnings from selling their property, they fell dead. But a certain man named Ananias, with Sapphira his wife, sold a possession and kept back part of the price, his wife also being privy to it, and brought a certain part, and laid it at the apostle's feet. But Peter said, "Ananias, why hath Satan filled thine heart to lie to the Holy Ghost, and to keep back part of the price of the land?" Acts 5:1-3

Make sure that when you do give, you give into good ground (kingdom work) with a cheerful heart. God loves a cheerful giver. 2 Corinthians 9:7 KJV

Sharing the good News of the Gospel is one of the greatest acts of love you can show another person. Some people don't think they are capable of sharing the Gospel. Many people see this as a job for the Pastor. Anyone can share their testimony of God's goodness as a way to win someone else. Simply sharing how God impacts your life and what Jesus did on Calvary, is called sowing a seed of faith. God can also use us to water the seed with words of encouragement from the Word. It is not your job to make the seed grow. That is the job of the Holy Spirit. We are instructed to tell people the good News. It's between them and God what happens after that.

And He said unto them, "Go ye into all the world, and preach the Gospel to every creature. He that believeth and is baptized shall be saved; but he that believeth not shall be damned. And these signs shall follow them that believe; in My Name shall they cast out devils; they shall speak with new tongues; they shall take up serpents; and if they drink any deadly thing, it shall not hurt them; they shall lay hands on the sick, and they shall recover." Mark 16:15-18 KJV

Some people have trouble giving. They have a take, take, take mentality. We have to remember that the world's system is not God's system. We all need to purpose in our lives to give to others. The Bible tells us that it is more blessed to give than it is to receive. When you give, you become a vessel that can receive again and again. Make room in your life to be used by God. Some people have trouble receiving. Knowing how to receive is a part of prosperity. We should always be gracious and grateful. Allow those who are led to bless you, to be a blessing. Pride is usually the reason people have trouble receiving. The Bible tells us that pride comes before a fall and that we should resist the proud.

When God delivered His people out of Egypt, He sent men in to spy out the promise land. Only two of them came back with a good report. God promised that the rest would not enter in. Our perspective should always be to see that *God is bigger than our problems*. A prostitute, Rehab, chose to believe that God was with the Israelites. She helped two of God's men by hiding them on her roof. That woman ended up in the genealogy of Jesus Christ. God is no respecter of persons. He makes Himself available to all who will believe in and obey Him.

Many people receive the Word into their heart and get saved. The angels in Heaven rejoice every time someone gives their life to the Lord. Sometimes, the seed that we sow needs to get watered and over time, the person comes to the knowledge of the truth of God's love. Don't be offended if you share the Gospel and someone rejects it. They are not rejecting you. They are rejecting Christ. Love is patient. Love is kind. Remember how patient God was with you. Pray for people and trust God to move on their hearts. Many of them have a choice to make, just like you did.

Don't think that little acts of kindness are insignificant. Jesus said when you give unto the least, you give unto Him. You could be the person to encourage our next great evangelist or leader. The most important gift we can share is our faith. You can use your journaling as a witnessing tool by encouraging others to use journaling, in addition to their normal Bible reading and prayer time, to enhance their relationship with the Lord. Teach people to write the vision.

And the Lord answered me, and said, write the vision, and make it plain upon tables, that he may run that reads it. Habakkuk 2:2 KJV

Write in your Journal about a person, who has made a difference in your life. Think about some ways you can make a difference in the lives of others. It may be a small thing or it may be something huge.

_____

_____

_____

_____

_____

_____

_____

_____

_____

Work on your long term goals. Keep it simple use B.A.S.E. as your reference point:

B-Be encouraged

A-Attach a promise from the Word

S-Stay focused

E-Enjoy your journey and encourage others

_____

_____

_____

_____

_____

_____

_____

_____

_____

_____

Chapter 18

Celebrate Your Victory

Having a 20/20 vision for your own life can be a bit scary. It's easy to look at others and determine changes that should be made, but what about your own life? Are you too close to the forest to see the trees that need pruning in your personal life? By now, you should have a vision for your life. Take your God given authority and walk into your destiny. You should have an honest assessment of the good, the bad and the ugly. Hopefully you have the desire to do whatever it takes to make the changes needed to reach your finish line. Run your race in your lane. God is not looking for swiftness, but for those who are willing to stay the course.

Real change only comes with God's help. Seek Him, while He may be found. We live in a dispensation of grace and time. Don't allow time to run out. Make today a day of sincere, heartfelt change in your life. God will meet you right where you are. You'll discover that God is good and wants to share good things with you. If you then, being evil, know how to give good gifts to your children, how much more will your Father who is in Heaven give what is good things to those who ask Him? KJV

When we love God, all things will work for our good. I realize that, for me walking by faith is to simply trust in God, knowing that He is more than able and willing to work all things out in my life. I also believe that in Romans 8:28, the verse states "to them that love God", the reader must understand that this is referring to loving God the way His Word teaches us to love. This is not the conditional standard of love that man has adopted, but the whole hearted love and reverence that our Heavenly Father deserves.

Being called according to His purpose, helped me to abandon my own agenda and seek, not just the hand of God, but the will and heart of God as well.

The fruit of the Spirit should be growing in our lives. Love, joy, peace, long suffering, gentleness, goodness, faith, meekness, and temperance: against such there is no law. Galatians 5:22-23 KJV

You are blessed to be a blessing. Stay motivated and encouraged. Help others obtain their miracles, while you're waiting for yours. The only limits to your victories in life are the ones you place on yourself. The vision God gives you will take you to the next level. Write the vision: Get who, the what, the when and the where written down. Make it plain. Write down how you plan to accomplish what's in your heart. Be sensitive to God's direction. It's called faith, because we won't always know every step, but we take steps in faith, trusting Him all the way. This shouldn't be about trying to put God in your agenda. We should be fully committed to His agenda. *Faith is our bridge from the natural to the supernatural.*

Be flexible in the transition times of life. When God says it's time to change, be ready and willing. I think some of the hardest times in life are when we have to do something we have never done before. There are also *blind times*, times where you may not have the answers you seek, but you have to simply trust God with childlike faith. We can sometimes get the "*what if*" syndrome. God has accounted for all the "what if's" in life. He has us covered. When we step out in faith and obedience, we soar like the eagles into God's perfect will for our lives. "

And all of us, as with unveiled face, [because we] continued to behold [in the Word of God] as in a mirror the glory of the Lord, are constantly being transformed into His very own Image in ever increasing splendor and from one degree of glory to another; [for this comes] from the Lord [who is] the Spirit. 2 Corinthians 3:18 AMP

The Apostle Paul had to make a transition in his life on the road to Damascus. He found himself confronted by the

Lord and changed, but he had to go through a *blind season.* He went through a waiting period and then had to enter into the fellowship of the other apostles. I'm sure they were nervous and so was he, but God raised him up to be one of the most powerful men of God in the Bible. And he fell to the earth and heard a voice saying unto him, "Saul, Saul, why persecutes thou me?" And he said, "Who are thou Lord?" And the Lord said, "I am Jesus, whom thou persecutes: it is hard for thee to kick against the pricks." And he trembling and astonished said, "Lord, what wilt thou have me to do?" And the Lord said, "Arise, and go into the city, and it shall be told thee what thou must do." And Saul arose from the earth; and when his eyes were opened, he saw no man, but they led him by the hand, and brought him into Damascus. Acts 9:6-8 KJV

Sometimes, transition means waiting. Elijah was instructed by the Lord to go to the brook, Cherith, and wait. In his season of waiting for further instruction, God sent the ravens to feed him meat and bread every day and he drank from the brook. One day, the brook dried up. The prophet Elijah had to wait for God's instructions before moving on. He ended up being sent to the house of a widow. Her son eventually died and Elijah was there to pray and revive him. If he had not obeyed God, he would have missed the opportunity to be used with the widow and her son. 1 Kings 17:1-7 Paraphrase KJV

One of the most important decisions a person can make is the choice about their salvation. It is a free gift that has to be accepted by choice. Another choice you can make is the way you perceive the people and events that happen around you. Look up. There is a Godly way to see every issue at hand. Choose to believe the revelation that God gives you, not the tribulation that the enemy may try to plant in your spirit. If my people who are called by My Name humble themselves and pray and seek My face, and turn from their evil ways, then I will hear from Heaven, forgive their sin, and heal their land." 2 Chronicles 7:14

Develop a healthy way to reward yourself for accomplishing short and long term goals. I like to go to the spa, have dinner at my favorite restaurant or take a trip. Journal three ways you would like to reward yourself. Make sure it's healthy and doesn't break your budget.

_____

_____

_____

_____

_____

_____

_____

Chapter 19

Maintenance

Your body is the temple of the Holy Spirit. We are a spirit, we have a soul, and we live in a body. We cannot neglect the care of any aspect of ourselves and expect to be our best for God. In addition to prayer and meditation, practical things like diet and exercise can play a part in being successful in accomplishing God's will for your life. Can you preach to the nations, sick? Can you give to the poor, if most of your income is spent on your medical bills? Symptoms may come. Remember, the Bible tells us that no weapon formed against you shall prosper. Anything that comes against you is from your enemy. God is for you. He is never against you. Health problems, financial lack, relationship issues can look like giants in our lives. We can overcome any giant with God on our side.

King David learned this lesson early in life. He went before the giant of the land with courage and boldness. The king could not find another man who was willing to go against the Philistine giant. David was younger than all his brothers, confident not in his own ability, but in the fact that God was with him. The Giant mocked David, who came to fight him with a sling shot. God used the faith that David had to defeat his enemy with one shot. We can be like David. What's a giant in your life? Tell it you come against it in the Name of the Lord and stand your ground.

By now, you should be able to reflect on your Journal entries and see a direction. Maybe you're ready to pursue a promotion, a new career path or even write a book. Perhaps, you have made some changes that will enhance your relationships and increase your finances. The possibilities are endless. My prayer for you is that whatever the Lord leads you to do, you do it with your whole heart, as unto the Lord.

One way to maintain the progress you've made, is to guard your heart. You can't allow yourself to be dragged back into wrong mindsets and bad habits. You can guard your heart by monitoring what you allow into your life. For example, I enjoy a good movie. Every year, I get a big group of family and friends together and we see the latest super hero movie. I love action and adventure, comedy and romance, but there are somethings I don't allow into my spirit. So as a rule of thumb, if you find that something upsets you, depresses you, angers you or arouses inappropriate feelings, let it go. Enjoy things that entertain with no bad side effects. I think Hollywood caters to what sells the most tickets. That's called smart business in the world, but if what sells tickets isn't edifying, it becomes a negative in your life. Many people complain about the direction the media is going in, but they watch it all. Give ratings to the types of things you love, not the things you love to complain about.

Stay accountable to God and yourself. Be sensitive to the teaching of your Pastors and spiritual leaders. Submit yourself to authority. Obey them that have the rule over you, and submit yourselves: for they watch for your souls, as they that must give account, that they may do it with joy, and not with grief: for that *is* unprofitable for you. Hebrews 13:17 KJV

Once you've achieved your short term goals, you should see a clear path to your long term goals. Remember to speak the Word of God over your life.

Once you decree a thing, it shall be established. Challenges will arise from time to time in life, but you are an overcomer. Barnabas was a Bible figure that I could relate to. He befriended the apostle Paul, when others were afraid to trust Paul and he evangelized with Paul. Barnabas and Paul disagreed about allowing John Mark to travel with them. Paul didn't trust John Mark, because of his previous actions. Barnabas and Paul disagreed so much, that they each went their own way. Acts 15:39 Paraphrase KJV

Barnabas took John Paul with him. Later, the Apostle Paul called for John Mark to come to him. Somewhere along the path, John Mark redeemed himself. I relate to Barnabas in allowing people to have a second chance. I've needed more than my share of do overs in life. Be a Barnabas to someone. God may use you to mentor someone with a great life purpose.

Learn not to look at your life through an out of focus lens. Journaling can equip you to see clearly the areas of your life that need to be adjusted and the areas that are working for you. Take your journaling serious, but make it a fun experience. Keep working toward your goals and continue to create new life goals. We are the handiwork of God. Be willing and ready to be used by God to fulfill your life purpose. My prayer is that you and I will one day hear the loving Voice of our Heavenly Father say, "Well done, good and faithful servant; you were faithful over a few things, I will make you ruler over many things. Enter into the joy of the Lord." Matthew 25:21

Journaling can be used as a stepping stone to define, reach and maintain your life goals. Adding Biblical principles to the process empowers you to be successful in fulfilling your life purpose and making a difference in the lives of others. Keep your vision in the forefront of your thinking. Where there is no vision the people perish. Proverbs 29:18 KJV

Be a visionary and start to think outside the box. Make a list of things to work toward for this week, this month, this year, 5 years, 20 years and even, 100 years. Develop a plan for your life that is realistic, obtainable and chartable. You can only do this effectively through the leading of the Lord. What is realistic in the world is different from what is realistic in the Lord. In the Will of God, we can do everything but fail! Goal setters, beware of setting goals that are unrealistic. For example, trying to be a millionaire by the end of the year when you first need to learn to tithe and balance your checkbook may be unrealistic. You may want to be married by next month and you're not even dating anyone. Nothing is impossible with God, but you won't accomplish anything of value without Him.

Charting progress determines things that enhance your life and the things that hold you back. After journaling for a short time, this should become clearer. Once you've identified the sabotaging behaviors, relationships and habits in your life, you can begin to make changes. Remember you are God's precious treasure. He gave His very best for you. Give Him your very best in life. However, we possess this precious treasure [the divine Light of the gospel] in [frail, human] vessels of the power may be shown to be from God and not from ourselves. 2 Corinthians 4:7 AMP

Reflect on your Chapter 7 Journal entries. Note your progress. Meditate on Scriptures that speak to your circumstances and remember, you are a work of art. You are God's masterpiece. Write about goals for healthy living. Separate your short and long term goals by category. Save your journaling notebooks. They can bring deep life insight to you, as you reflect on previous journal entries.

_____

_____

_____

_____

_____

_____

_____

_____

_____

Chapter 20

Process to Promotion

The first thing that comes to my mind when I drive onto the grounds of my church or any other place of worship, is the obedience of the Pastors. It took faith, hard work, commitment and obedience to establish such a beautiful, anointed place to worship. My Pastors occasionally tell the story of their humble beginnings in a small store front. Now, they Pastor a beautiful, large church with over 1,200 members. Don't despise the small steps it takes to get to big places in life.

I can only imagine the process they had to go through, the obstacles that they faced and the naysayers that tried to discourage them. Yet, they remained determined, steadfast and faithful in their pursuit of God's purpose and plan for their lives. I sometimes wonder what would be in the place of my church if my Pastors had failed to obey God. Would there be a Super Wal-Mart there instead? Would million dollar homes have been developed there? Would it have remained a wooded lot? I thank God for obedient believers who press through circumstances to achieve the vision God has put down on the inside of them.

Pressing through process will always result in a promotion. Choosing to follow the plan of God for your life is choosing life. Sometimes people make excuses for not obeying God. When God asked Moses to go get His people out of their bondage in Egypt, Moses said he was not a good communicator. Moses said to the Lord, "Pardon your servant, Lord. I have never been eloquent, neither in the past, nor since you have spoken to your servant. I am slow of speech and tongue." Exodus 4:10 NIV

God went on to remind Moses of who made his mouth. I can relate to Moses. When God called me to ministry, I had a list of reasons why that wouldn't work. I felt, shy, awkward, I had struggles with depression and low self-esteem. Why on earth would God want to use someone like me for anything? I had a heart for the things of God, but limited myself in my own thinking. God had entrusted me with a heart for His people for a reason. One thing that I could not deny in my life was that I was, and still am a compassionate person. I care about God's people. Now don't get me wrong, this doesn't qualify me to minister. What qualifies me is the Blood of Jesus and obeying the call. Many are called, but few are chosen." NKJ

Obedience is a big deal to God. Don't miss your moment. Obey God in all things. In order to be used by God, one must have a willing and obedient heart. If a person is willing to serve others and is obedient to do what the spirit of God instructs them, then they can be used mightily. If you're just willing, but never obedient, you are deceived. If you are truly willing, obedience will be the end result. In saying that, I must clarify that God is God and can use anything or anyone as He sees fit. He used a donkey to give a message. He used a burning bush to talk to Moses. He used a prostitute to hide the Israelite men. He can use us. The level of use is determined by how **willing** and **obedient** we are. You won't be willing or obedient without faith. But without faith it's impossible to please Him: for he that cometh to God must believe that He is, and that He is a rewarder of them that diligently seek him. Hebrews 11:6 KJV

God equips whoever He calls. My fears were irrational fears planted by the enemy from my youth. Sexual abuse, depression, low self-esteem and the root of rejection were giants in my life. As a child, I felt unlovable, and even thought God didn't like me. God is never the source of any problem. He is the problem solver. Each giant fell hard and bowed to the Name of the Lord Jesus, because of God's love and mercy. "No weapon formed against thee shall prosper, and every tongue which rises against you in judgment, you shall condemn. This is the heritage of the servants of the

Lord, and their righteousness is from Me." says the Lord. Isaiah 54:17 NKJ

The Word makes it clear. We wrestle not against flesh and blood, but against principalities, against powers, against the rulers of darkness of this world, against spiritual wickedness in high places. Ephesians 6:12 KJV

Be willing to go through whatever process God has for your restoration. The Bible shows us many examples of people going through a process for their deliverance. There was a blind man who had to have spit and dirt mixed up by Jesus and then put onto his eyes. There was a king who had to go dip in the pool of Bethesda. Be willing to do what it takes for a breakthrough! God will restore the years the cancer worm has stolen. (Joel 2:25 paraphrase KJV)

Lifestyle of Prayer

The start of your prayer life begins with the most important prayer you'll ever pray, the sinner's prayer. If you want to be sure that you have a place in the Lamb's Book of Life, start by praying this prayer;

Father God, I believe in my heart and confess with my mouth that Jesus is the Son of God. I accept Jesus as my personal Lord and Savior. I repent of all my sin and ask You to come into my heart and make me new. In Jesus name, I pray. Amen.

The Bible tells us to pray without ceasing. Spend time in daily prayer. Allow God to use you to bring positive change to your life and the lives of those around you. Surely your goodness and love will follow me all the days of my life, and I will dwell in the house of the Lord forever. Psalm 23: 6 NIV

Let goodness and love catch you! Don't get ahead of God's plan for your life and don't lag behind. Walk with God and obey God to experience the abundant life He has for you. Stay blessed and encouraged.

About the Author

Author, Stephanie Daniels grew up in New York and moved to Virginia as a teenager. She earned her Bachelor's degree in Psychology from Liberty University. Stephanie also studied at Faith Landmarks Bible Institute. Stephanie has authored books, such as Grace Growing Up and Overcoming Eve. She has also written for several magazines, including The Mnemosyne, Glory Christian Magazine and The Examiner. Stephanie can be contacted on Facebook or at writethevision101@gmail.com. Look for Stephanie's next series of books on the *family*, coming soon!

References: Speak The Word By: Marilyn Hickey and Sarah

Bowling (Booklet)

Made in the USA
Lexington, KY
19 May 2017